# IF YOU WANT TO BE RICH, DON'T WORK FOR MONEY

## David O.

# CONTENTS

# INTRODUCTION: THERE IS NO SPOON

In the late 1990s and early 2000s, Hollywood released a movie trilogy that began with The Matrix. It depicts a futuristic dystopia where people live in two worlds—a computer simulation known as "the Matrix," and the real world.

The main character, Neo, had powers to alter reality in the Matrix world. While learning how to use his powers, he met a young child who also had this gift of bending reality.

The child held a spoon in his hand and was able to bend it in all directions just by looking at it. Neo was curious. Then the young child told him the secret:

"There is no spoon."

As long as you think you are holding a spoon, it will be impossible for you to bend it however you want. But the moment you understand that there actually is no spoon, the possibilities are endless.

Neo took the spoon from the young child, focused on it, and reminded himself, "There is no spoon." Instantly, Neo could bend the spoon any way he chose.

This is the same idea I hope to communicate with you concerning money. Becoming very rich is like bending the spoon. As long as you think there is a spoon, it is impossible to bend the spoon. As long as you think money is real, you will be unsuccessful in bending the spoon.

But the moment you understand that there is no spoon, that money is not real, you become capable of bending the spoon in any direction you want.

This is the main object of this book. Keep that thought at the base of your mind as you read every word. Your ability to create wealth for yourself is founded upon the understanding that money is not real.

And money is indeed not real. You will come to understand this when you read how central banks print money in Chapter 4.

Your feelings should not be linked to how much money is in your bank account. So if you are sad or angry because you have no money, remember that money is not real.

Similarly, you can choose to smile if you see $120 million in your bank account balance. But in the end, it doesn't matter because there is no spoon.

I know your logical mind is arguing with me right now. You are counting out all the things you could do if you had that much money in your bank account. But that is why you are where you are financially! You are waiting to have the money so that you can do what you want. That is where the problem is.

You see, money is not real. There is no spoon. As long as you are waiting for the money to come before you do what you want, whether that be financial goals or more personal aims, you will never achieve anything significant.

Yes, you need money to get it done. But money is not a thing. It is not even real. You will not be able to bend the spoon if you think you are holding a spoon. You can only bend the spoon when you realize that there is no spoon.

How much money do you need to start a billion-dollar project? The answer is zero. But where is the money going to come from? The answer is: wherever the money is right now.

This may sound a bit far-fetched to you now. But when you are through with this book, you will not only understand that money is not real, you will also know how to make any amount you want available.

I have spent a significant part of my adult life studying the subject of money and how some people have come to amass a lot of it. There are entrepreneurs who are fortunate to be at the right place at the right time with the right skills (or ideas). Two examples are Larry Page and Sergey Brin of Google.

But there are others who are not really lucky. They don't have the skill. They missed great opportunities. And they still ended up very rich and successful. Most of them are not really famous. An example is Bill Gross the CEO of Idealab who has started more than 100 companies and had a lot of failures.

This book is all about the ideas that will position you for the best of both worlds. Let this book inspire you to do something.

# PART I: MONEY IS NOT REAL

Then I asked how much it cost. They said 14 years

and 6 months. So I paid money instead.

# CHAPTER 1: WORKING HARDER WON'T MAKE YOU RICH

**M**ost people in this world are programmed to be slaves of money. I used to think the programming started from preschool. But I was wrong. The programming often begins at conception.

A lot of families begin before the parents are ready to take up parenting responsibilities. And being born into that financial insecurity kills the self-esteem of those kids before they can even spell their names.

And generally, most children grow up in middle- and working-class families. What do you think those parents instill in their kids as they grow up? The very same ideas of working for money.

Neuroscientists tell us that for the first 7 years of our lives, our brains are recording information from our environment, to learn how to behave from the world and people around us. After age 7, choices have already been instilled in our minds. Our comfort zone has already been set. You can tell with 80% accuracy what the child is going to grow up to be and what the child won't be.

It is easy to fight these facts, but if you look critically at your life, you will discover it to be true. Your preferences are not really yours. Someone passed them on to you. And those inclinations might be the very thing holding you back from becoming successful. Think about it.

◆ ◆ ◆

Why do we go to school? First, to learn how to read and write. Then, to learn something that will make us qualified to have a job. Have you noticed that schools don't teach about money? And that is on purpose.

Of course, they "teach" business and entrepreneurship. And yes, they teach accounting. But let me ask you a simple question: do you learn how to drive a car by reading a book and taking a test?

No. You learn to drive by driving. You learn to surf by surfing. Now imagine if your driving instructor doesn't drive, and learned how to drive from a book. Or maybe she drove twice 13 years ago and crashed once, took multiple written exams, and then became qualified to be a tutor.

Would you allow such a person to teach you how to drive? But that is what our school system is based on. We started out having real teachers, in elementary school. We had teachers who read every day teach us how to read. We had teachers who write every day teach us how to write. But, gradually and surely, we started having teachers who don't practice what they teach.

And guess what? We become like them. We start thinking like

them. We start reading to learn instead of doing to learn. Reading is for acquiring knowledge. And I am not against that. You will always have reasons to read from time to time. You are reading this book, as an example.

However, you cannot learn without practice. The information of this book will be useless to you if you don't do something with it.

◆ ◆ ◆

This mindset of working for money is the way most of us are wired, because that's the way we have been conditioned. The only exception is if you are from a wealthy family or you had a more challenging childhood.

We believe we are lucky when we get a job that pays us something that barely meets our living expenses. We cut our coats according to our salaries. We shape our expectations according to which rung of the career ladder we are on.

We believe in step-by-step growth. It is what school got us used to. And when we see the anomalies and outliers strike it big, we make up a fact that explains why they can do it but we can't.

So we just stick to what we know. And what do we know? Working harder. The things we want, we work for. It gets so bad that people see money in terms of time.

"I can't afford that right now. I have to be earning 4x my current pay. And I have to be a senior executive to earn that. And I can't be a senior executive for another 6 years." Yada, yada, yada.

That is what the school system instills in the mind: work

harder. But let me break it to you; working hard won't make you rich. Working harder won't make you rich. I know this is contrary to conventional wisdom, but it is true.

You need hard work to stay rich, not to get rich. If you get rich and you don't work hard (and smart), you will lose a lot of your wealth (if not everything). But when getting started, hard work is not the way forward.

◆ ◆ ◆

I hope you can begin to see how this lines up. If something has a price, you can have it if you choose to. You don't need any qualifications to afford anything. Stop translating money into effort. Money is money. Effort is effort.

If it costs $10 million, just take that number at its surface value. That is not 40 years of work saving almost 50% every month. Stop thinking of how you can afford your dream with your current salary.

Many people dream according to their budget. They have to see the price of something before they know whether they like it or not. What a sad way to live!

It is easy when your dream house costs $1M and you earn $50K per year. You know you will have to step up. But the real problem is if you are earning $120K per year (which is a fortune in your eyes) and you find a house you love, only to be told it is $56M. You may even become angry. This is because you expect your reward for hard work to fit your dream.

Money is money. Don't give it any other meaning. It is just a figure. It is no longer even a reward. You will get to know more as you read along.

But I hope I have been able to convince you that the rich life you want will not be a reward or consequence of your work. Working harder won't make you rich.

Work is work; money is money. Time is time; money is money. Time is not equivalent to money. At least, that is the way the rich think.

# CHAPTER 2: THE RICH DON'T WORK FOR MONEY

I am not the first person to say these things. These concepts are not new. People just take notice of these things in different ways. And there are those who get excited about a new idea, but they soon forget what it is all about. Then they are back to their usual lives.

The journey to wealth is scary. There is nothing that is safe and secure here. Nothing! If you want safety and security, then you will continue to get walked over as an employee. I am not against the "employee" life. But if you are working at your job primarily because of the money they pay you, you are in slavery.

The mindset of this book is not about being an entrepreneur. Instead, it is about using the entrepreneurial mindset to achieve financial success. You can still continue working where you do if you like it, but you won't be dependent on it for money.

◆ ◆ ◆

What do you do if you don't have money? For most people, they look for a job. Now, that is what the rich don't do. Just like I said, the journey to riches is neither safe nor secure.

Prioritizing being safe and secure has a cost. And the cost is: control. The control is out of your hands. To the rich, if there is no control, then it is neither safe nor secure.

If you want to be rich, you have to understand that control equals "safe and secure." And a job is just the opposite of that. There are too many uncertainties that can take that job (or income source) away from you. And you won't be able to do anything about it.

So what do the rich do when they don't have money? It is very simple—they go where the money is and figure stuff out.

You have probably heard the phrase many times—the rich don't work for money, money works for the rich. But have you ever asked, before the rich had money, *how* was money working for them?

The mindset of the rich is to prioritize control from the very onset. It is not about making money first; instead, it is about understanding how money works. Or, in most cases, it is about understanding how a particular business works.

How does it really work? How is money made in the industry? Who makes the big money? Where and when is the real deal made? Those are the questions of the rich. They put their minds to work and figure stuff out.

This is the reason the first set of people to understand a newly created industry become billionaires. They figure it out before everybody else. And hence they have the advantage.

If it took working for free to figure stuff out, the rich would do it. They would humble themselves to the dust of the ground just to understand how the business (or money) works. And once they do understand, they throttle down.

Now you know that working harder won't make you rich. You also know that working for money won't make you rich. What makes you rich is figuring stuff out: going where the money is and figuring things out.

Where do you need to go? Where do you need to start going every day? What are you going to figure out? Make a decision.

# CHAPTER 3: 7 THINGS RICH PEOPLE ADVISE BUT NEVER DO

W atch what rich people do, not what they say.

The world is divided into two. There are the rich and the poor. The rich are those who have money work for them. The poor are those who work for money.

In many people's eyes, to be poor is to be the beggar by the street who can't afford anything. But that is an extreme case of poverty. If you trade your time for money in the bid to afford the good things of life, you are likewise not among the rich.

The middle class is a category designed to soothe people who are hardworking. It is possible to join the rich from being in the middle class. But it is quite rare. Remember, the true definition of the rich is someone who doesn't work for money but who money works for. And, of course, they make plenty of money to boot.

You can work to have fulfillment. And everybody needs that. But if your primary motivation for work is the pay, then you are definitely playing the poor man's game. The key is to think differently about work, life, and money.

Our society glorifies rich people. They often get turned into thought leaders of some sort. Yes, it is true they have some wisdom, but they often mislead the public. They give advice that they don't follow or won't follow.

If you want to be rich, don't do what rich people say. Instead, watch what they do. Study their life stories. Look for the moments they made a big leap and see what they did and how they did it. This will tell you about the actual steps.

There is a lot of advice rich people give that they don't take or never took themselves. Here are 7 of them:

## 1. Save Money

The rich don't save money. The reason they will tell you is that they have a lot of money so they don't have to save. But that is not the real reason. The real reason is that saving money is not a smart financial decision.

Currently in Germany (as an example), you pay the bank to keep your money in it. They don't pay you any interest. In other places, the interest is so low that the value of your money depreciates in value faster than the interest can keep up. So by the time you get your money back, it can do way less than what it could before you saved it.

The rich don't save money. The rich invest money. They buy assets and investments. The only benefit of saving is the self-discipline it teaches. Be smart.

## 2. Reduce Spending

This sounds smart, but it is just as bad as the advice to save money. When things are tough, the conventional advice is to reduce spending. There is only one problem. If you reduce spending, everybody will believe that you are going broke. And that leads to another problem.

Business people become scared to do business with you. Nobody wants to jump onto a sinking ship. Negotiating deals becomes unnecessarily difficult. They won't expressly tell you why they are hesitant.

But if you throw an extravagant party or demonstrate wealth in some form, they flock to you with deals. This is the way of the wealthy. Only poor people cut down spending.

I have always thought about the reason wealthy people throw crazy expensive parties. It is not for anything but to show their strong hand in business negotiation.

## 3. Get Out of Debt

Rich people don't think the way poor people do. Poor people are trying to get out of debt while rich people are trying to get into more debt. To the poor, debt is a burden. To the rich, debt is a financial instrument.

Rich people use money to make money. And where do you think they get the initial money they start with? From a job? Far from it! They often get it from a loan. They get into debt.

The difference is that poor people use debts to purchase liabilities. A liability is something that doesn't make money and depreciates with time. An example is taking a loan out to buy a car just because the monthly payment seems affordable.

## 4. Go to School

A great number of super-rich people in the world are people who flunked school. The likes of Bill Gates, Kanye West, and Michael Dell. Of course, they all had some form of schooling, but they knew when to quit school. Those who keep enrolling in school after school never break into the wealthy circles.

There are some schools people go to for the association. But the majority of people keep learning and are always afraid to turn the knowledge into something tangible in the real world. And there is no school like the real world.

In life, experience is king. What you know from books is different from what you know from experience. The best advice is to get out in the real world and make mistakes. If you can read, write, speak, and you have a basic knowledge of the skill you want to work with, you have had enough school.

## 5. Get a Job

Rich people don't get rich by having a job. They get rich by having a business or investments. There is nothing wrong with having a job if that job is what you want. But when someone is advising you on going forward, they only tell you to get a job because they think you can't stomach being on your own.

Rich people work to learn and be fulfilled. They work to get exposed to opportunities. They don't work because they want money. If money is what you want, a job won't give that to you.

## 6. Diversify

Unless they are an investment expert, I can't think of any rich person who diversifies. They all put all their eggs in one basket and guard it with an armored tank. Those who diversify clearly don't know what to do with money.

Rich people put their money in what they understand and have a reasonable amount of control over. Poor people, on the other hand, get enticed by the next big thing and the idea of diversification. People who deal in real estate don't do stocks. Those who do stocks don't do real estate (except when they are buying their own home).

This is the way true rich people are. But when giving advice to the general public, they tell you to diversify because you are not deeply knowledgeable in any area. So, it is the safest advice.

## 7. Take Vacations

The rich don't go on vacation. When they travel, there is always some business tied to the trip one way or another. They make vacations out of business trips. When they travel for leisure, their eyes are always opened for business opportunities in that area.

Poor people take vacations to run away from work. And they avoid thinking about anything related to work by all means. However, rich people can't stop themselves from getting into business mode wherever they go.

It is all about loving what you do for work.

There are a lot of other things rich people say but don't do. But I have picked these 7 because they are easy mindset changes to start off with. I hope it straightens out your thinking.

# CHAPTER 4: HOW CENTRAL BANKS CREATE MONEY FROM THIN AIR

This is going to be an oversimplified version of quantitative easing, something everybody can easily understand. So, let's get right into it.

## The Basic Definition

Quantitative easing is quite simply a process whereby the central bank injects more cash into the economy by buying off debts (bad debts, in most cases) with cash that didn't exist prior.

To understand better, let us use an illustration.

Clara buys a toy from Daisy for $100. Clara paid $50 and took on a debt of $50 (which she agreed to pay in installments). The economy goes down and Clara cannot afford her payments to Daisy anymore. Also, the toy is now worth $20. So, Bruno comes to save Clara.

Clara transfers the ownership of the toy to Bruno. But she still gets to play with it. Bruno then writes a check to Daisy (on

Clara's behalf) to pay off the complete $50 debt on the toy. But there is a problem: Bruno doesn't have any money.

However, Bruno has authority. Whatever Bruno calls money is money. All Bruno needs to do is to write "$50" with a pen on a piece of toilet paper and give it to Daisy. Daisy can then spend this however she wants.

If anyone ever challenges Daisy about the toilet paper with "$50" written on it, she only has to say, "Bruno gave it to me." And it will be accepted. Nobody dares to go against Bruno's wishes.

In this scenario, Bruno is the central bank. Clara is the company (or entity) that needs saving during an economic downturn. Daisy is the commercial bank or investment bank, etc.

Now, this is where things go crazy. There are cases where Daisy and Clara are the same entities. An example of this is when banks take money to pay off a debt they owe themselves in a recession to avoid going bankrupt. In fact, this case is the most common. And the complications can go on and on.

If there is an economic downturn, how does Bruno choose who he helps? Certainly, Bruno doesn't help everybody. Bruno only helps the big ones, those whose failure will cause a significant dent to society. The big ones are expected to help the smaller ones, but they often choose not to and get away with it.

## The Central Banks

There are 5 top central banks in the world that control the economy and monetary policy of the 5 countries or constituencies where they are based. They are:

- Federal Reserve Bank of America (United States)
- Bank of England (England)
- European Central Bank (EU)
- Bank of Japan (Japan)
- People's Bank of China (China)

These are the big Brunos in the world. Interestingly, they are not controlled by the government. They are accountable (sort of) to the government but they are not subject to the government.

Let's talk about the Federal Reserve Bank—or the Fed—in the United States, since it deals with the largest economy and leads all the other central banks.

## The Fed

The Fed in the United States was created in 1913 in response to the financial turbulence the country had experienced in the years leading up to it. The Fed was created when the act passed the US Congress (and was signed into law by President Wilson) in December 1913. But the real mastermind creation happened in 1910 when a couple of bankers had a secret meeting on Jekyll Island. The meeting was made public later after the creation of the Fed, revealing that the idea of a central bank created wasn't by politicians but by bankers.

In 1971, President Nixon took the US dollar off the gold standard, hence undercutting the rest of the world who had their currencies pegged to the US dollar. This event is known as the Nixon Shock.

The US dollar currency was basically a gold certificate before 1971. You were originally able to redeem physical gold with the currency. But then in August 1971, when President Nixon made the announcement to take the US dollar off the gold standard, there was already a law prohibiting individuals from owning gold. (That law was later repealed in 1974.)

What is the implication of this? Before, if the United States wanted to create a $20 note, they had to ensure that they had the gold equivalent in their reserve.

Since Nixon's announcement in 1971, the United States has been able to print money as they wish to. The currency is no longer pegged to anything but the might and reputation of the USA. Think about it this way:

It costs about 15.4 cents (value) to print a $100 bill.

Most other countries have their currencies pegged to the US dollar through the Bretton Woods Agreement. And so, the agreement had to fail. This basically turned central banks into printing presses.

Since 1971, the US dollar has been free-falling in value. The price of gold right now is about $1,648 per ounce. And you can check the real-time price of gold whenever you are reading this. Of course, the price of gold has generally been on the rise since 1971. An ounce of gold used to be $35.

The emphasis today is not on how much gold is in the Federal

Reserve vault. Instead, it is on how much debt is in their balance sheet. That tells you how much the world has changed.

## The 2008 Event

The US economy tumbled in 2008 after experiencing amazing highs in 2006. There are several explanations for what really happened. But the chief of the matter has to do with subprime mortgages (loans). Apparently, too many loans that shouldn't have been given were given. And it created bad debt.

Bad debt is debt that the debtor has defaulted in paying. And the underlying asset for the loan has lost so much value that it doesn't make sense to sell it. Even if there is an attempt to sell it, there is no available buyer.

This happened with the real estate market in 2008. And the Fed rushed in to save the day. Over $1.4 trillion was printed to save the economy from the 2008 crisis.

In other words, Bruno chooses who he helps and writes out more numbers on more toilet paper.

So, how does it affect you?

## How Quantitative Easing Affects You

Assume you have $50 (in the down market) and you are the richest guy on the street in Bruno's territory. The moment Daisy (who is also Clara in most cases) takes Bruno's check (the $50 written on toilet paper) to a shop, the shop owner takes the money instantly and promises to deliver the merchandise in the future. Hence, the shop owner becomes as rich as you are overnight.

Gradually everyone will know that there is another rich man on the street. Your wholesalers will see that and create a demand competition between you and the shop owner (even though the supply hasn't changed).

Before, their only demand was coming from you because you were the only one rich enough to buy from them. Now that the shop owner has $50 too, demand has gone up and hence they will increase their price to level the playing field. And the ripple effect will go through the economy until it reaches the smallest item.

Therefore, your $50 can no longer do what it could. It can no longer buy what it could. It has been devalued.

The interesting part of this is not that the shop owner is now as rich as you. Instead, it is that the money is not a result of work done or value created. It was money that Bruno created. What does this mean?

## The New Laws of Money

Before quantitative easing was possible, money was a reward for value creation. However, since quantitative easing became a reality, money is no longer a reward for value created.

If you continued to see money as a reward for value created, you would continue to be that rich man on Bruno's street seeing the value of your money drop further down.

You can try hard to create more value and get paid for it, but Bruno can write numbers on toilet paper faster. And, in most cases, he will.

The new law of money is to use created money to create value.

Knowing who Bruno is and what he is capable of, it is better to get your hands on as much of his toilet paper money as you can and use it to create value for society.

Instead of being paid as a reward for creating value, you get paid as an incentive to create value. This is the new law of money. And this is what our society runs on today.

## Today's Reality

As I write this, the world is in the middle of a serious health challenge: a contagious virus, COVID-19, that has crippled the business community. The economy is down everywhere. And Bruno is flying in again to save the day.

Can you see what is happening? The stimulus packages that various governments have announced that they are injecting into the economy, guess where they are coming from? Bruno.

I do not consider this system unfair because I don't like it (and, honestly, I don't like it at all). I consider it unfair because there is no formal education about it.

Myriads of people still hope to earn a living by working hard every day for money (because of how they were trained in school).

This is how the financial world works now. What are you going to do about it?

# CHAPTER 5: MONEY IS NOT REAL, THERE ARE ONLY DECISIONS

Entrepreneurship is a show business. As much as it entails hard work, know-how, and several skills, it is ultimately successful depending on how good the show is. If you don't understand the show business, you will keep losing and not know why.

When I started saying about myself that "I am rich," people thought I was making a positive affirmation, that I meant it in a symbolic way. But now, when I say "I am rich," people believe I have millions in my bank account.

What changed? Not much. I just had things to show. If I told someone there was no money in my bank account, they wouldn't believe me. And I would never say that because there is always money there!

Nobody wants to do business with a poor man. An investor once said, "If you come to me to ask for money, you better come looking like money." There is a difference between being rich and giving the perception that you are rich. However, nobody sees it and, quite frankly, nobody really cares.

You need to look rich to be rich. The big secret of life is to look like who you want to become. Look like it, talk like it, walk like it, and gesture like it. The world is too lazy to tell the difference. And the world is not looking for the one who is aspiring. Rather, the world is looking for the one who has become.

As you can see from the last chapter, money is now an idea. It is no longer real. More of it can be created in a snap of a finger, just like that. And they can also make it disappear. There are all kinds of things that can make money disappear. One of them is the opposite of quantitative easing, known as quantitative tightening.

This is the reason the world is being pushed towards a cashless society. Money becomes a bunch of figures on a computer screen. Then, it can be properly tweaked at will. But even now, it is no longer real. The central bank may not determine your pay, but they determine what its value is.

The #1 skill of an entrepreneur is raising money. This is quite different from fundraising. Fundraising is about raising money for charity works. But raising money as an entrepreneur requires the ability to source and get the money required to execute a project at hand.

The problem of poor people is that they don't have a big (for-profit) project. If you do have such a project, all you need to do is to look rich and go ask for the money required from people who have that kind of money to invest. Another problem with poor people is that they keep asking for money from broke people like themselves.

Money is not real. The thing that is real are decisions. I decided to write and publish this book. I didn't have all the resources I would need to execute that when I started writing it. But I made a decision to do it. And if this book is in your hands today, it means I succeeded.

This is how everything else is. You make the decision to do something and all the resources will come to you if you are resolute enough about getting it done. Anything is possible, you just have to be stubborn enough to believe in your goals in the face of daunting challenges.

But if you don't believe in your dream or project, don't expect anyone else to believe in it. Your problem is not money. Money is not real. Your problem (if you have one) is that you don't have a big project you have made up your mind to do. You have not made a decision about what to do. Make a decision today.

◆ ◆ ◆

It is said that successful people make decisions very fast and change them very slowly (if they ever change them). Average people make decisions very slowly and change them very fast.

Poor people don't make decisions, life kicks them about. They spend their lives reacting.

If I know how you make decisions, I can predict with fair accuracy whether you will be successful or not. You can think and plan all you want, but the world belongs to the action-takers.

◆ ◆ ◆

If you say you have a dream or project and are still poor, then your problem is raising money. You don't know how to convince people to give you money. And raising money is very simple.

Raising money means giving people the perception that what they hope to get from you in return is greater than the value of the money they invest. You need to know what they want and how they want it. If they have any doubts, you won't get the money. They must be more willing to give you the money than you are willing to take it.

There are 3 basic things people who have money look at to make their decision of whether to invest in your project. The first is how you look. You need to give the perception that you are rich and that their money is no big deal to you. The second is your competence for what you want to do with the money. This means your skill and experience. If you are not super-competent, there must be someone on your team who is super-competent. And that person must follow you to the meeting where you ask for the money.

The third is your future. This is why tech VCs love people in their 20s. Nobody wants to put money into something you will do part-time. They want to put money on something you will spend your life on.

Show them a good picture of these three traits and you will get the money. If they are still hesitating after you demonstrate these, it is either because they don't have the money or you are talking to the wrong person (a.k.a. not the decision-maker).

Money is not real. Create your dream and raise the money you need. The money you want is in the hands of someone else. You only have to find that person and convince them. It could be a bank manager, VC, investor, etc. You are just one decision away from the money you want.

Money is not real. Decide and the money will appear.

# PART II: THE MINDSET OF THE RICH

"You can't be rich overnight," says someone who doesn't understand what happened in 1971, 2008, and 2020.

# CHAPTER 6: IF YOU WANT TO BE RICH, DON'T WORK FOR MONEY

The rich don't work for money. They don't get paid for the work (or hard work) they do.

Maybe you know someone who works for money and earns a lot. It doesn't matter how much they earn, it will come to an end. And they are not really earning much if you put the amount in some serious perspective.

Working for money will only make you a high-income earner at best. That doesn't make people rich. Many sports players and entertainers today are high-income earners. And most go broke after their careers are over. Even while they are still earning big, they pay huge taxes and spend their money on things that only increase their taxes.

These high-income earners might look like the rich, but they are not. If you have followed my discourse thus far, you will understand that my definition of a rich person is not a high-income earner.

The income of the rich is not a reward for any work. Rather, it is a system set up to produce income even while you sleep. If you can't make money while you sleep, it means you will work like a mule until you die.

Work ought to be fulfilling. But the game of money is completely different. The hardest-working people often have the least money. And as long as you think that you have to earn money through work, you will never have a lot of money.

Big money is not earned, it is made. Even top bankers and hedge fund managers don't earn a lot in salaries. The highest-earning head of a central bank in the world is the governor of the Bank of England. And he earns just about $1.14M in a year. Most others earn much less. Just for some perspective, his US counterpart earns about $203K in a year. And you know there are properties that are $20M, $50M, $100M, and above. This goes to show you that compensation for work (even smart work) is not the way to riches.

Rich people have businesses. Rich people have money working for them. Rich people play the game of money. Rich people work, but they don't work for money.

## Dependence on a Paycheck Creates Poverty

The problem with a paycheck is that it blocks you from thinking straight. People are mentally bound to how much they earn. This is why they require a mindset shift before they can move from one income level to another.

Rich people think of how to create wealth. They think of how to create a fountain that perpetually produces money for them.

But poor and middle-income people just want to satisfy today's needs. They don't want to think about tomorrow.

The money game is played with the mind. When a person's mind is conditioned to their paycheck, they don't see the need to create a business or have other income streams. Their paycheck continues to be their solace until the day it stops coming.

The concept of retirement plans gives people the idea that their paycheck will keep coming as long as they live. They never think about what they can do if there is no paycheck.

The paycheck is a mental limitation. It is a factor that keeps people from what they can do. Most people don't think unless their backs are against the wall.

## Don't Trade Your Future Millions for Today's Pennies

One of the basic differences between the rich and everybody else is that the rich play the long game. Most people only think short-term. Many live from month to month.

If you want to play the long game and win, then you must be prepared to deal with losses in the short-term. These losses involve walking away from instant benefit in favor of the greater benefits after a decade.

There are deals and transactions that result in instant benefits. But if that is all a person takes part in, it is almost impossible to get rich. Multiple millions and billions are built over the long-term. They are grown over several years, and in some cases, over several decades.

Always think about the worth of what you are involved in. In 10 years, what will it be worth? Trust me, 10 years can pass by quickly. The only thing that will let you get ahead in 10 years are the things you do differently today.

Give yourself the chance to grow wealth for at least a decade. Don't burn all your future prospects. Don't trade your future millions for a few bucks today.

## Fix Your Gaze on the Big Wave

An alarming thing happens when you are just focused on the paycheck. Big money moves will be happening all around you and you won't notice. Your mind will just be narrowed in on that paycheck.

The moment the paycheck is taken away from you and you have to fend for yourself in the wild business world, you will be surprised at how much you never saw before.

Unless your gaze is on the big wave, you will miss the real opportunities. If your concern is only on the short-term reward for your hard work, you won't get rich. Rich people learn to take their eyes away from their immediate compensation.

If your eyes are fixed on the immediate compensation, you will not see the big picture. If you don't see the big picture, you will miss obvious opportunities.

Take an example of two construction workers hired to work on a massive resort in an average town. One is fixed on the amount he earns per day for his work. The other is thinking about the changes that will happen to the town when the resort is completed in two years.

One worker is thinking of how he can get the construction company to increase his wages. But the other worker is thinking of how he can benefit from the changes the resort will bring to the town. This second worker (who is thinking about the future) will find a way to buy property nearby. He can even write to big companies to be their official partner in the small town to sell their products. There are myriads of things he can do.

10 years after the construction of the resort, the first worker is looking for another construction company to hire him. Meanwhile, the second worker is a major business-man in the (now) big town that used to be average.

Keep your eyes on the big picture.

## Work for Free and Figure Stuff Out

The story of Robert Kiyosaki, author of *Rich Dad Poor Dad*, always comes to my mind. When he wanted to learn about money he went to his best friend's dad, who told young Robert to work for free.

His best friend's dad was an entrepreneur, and he understood the difference between an employee and an entrepreneur. He said to young Robert, "**The moment I start paying you, you start thinking like an employee**."

So Robert agreed to work for free and learn about money. But then he asked his best friend's dad, "So how am I going to make money if I work for free?" Then the man gave a beautiful answer: **"That's the stuff you figure out."**

The rich mindset is the entrepreneurial mindset that figures stuff out.

Working for free already puts you in a tight position. It forces you to think. Yes, you have to make money, but not as compensation for your hard work. How am I going to make this work?

Figure things out and grow rich.

## Position, Position, Position

The 3 most important things in real estate investing are location, location, location. In growing wealth, it's position, position, position.

Your position determines a lot of things by default. People will only offer what you look like you can handle. Also, your position determines how much seriousness and attention will be given to what you propose.

It is always good to position oneself as highly competent as possible. Positioning is the big secret of the business world. I have seen two people doing the same thing and one person is paid double what the other person gets. Interestingly, both of them are ladies and the role was in Human Resources. The one being paid double had working experience in another company before the company hired her. The other one was fresh from school. They were nearly the same age.

Positioning is not merely to do with appearance. It is in the people, things, and places you choose to associate with.

## Learn How to Sell

If you are going to be rich, you've got to learn how to sell. Even if you are not going to be an entrepreneur, you have to at least know how to sell yourself.

Selling is about making people buy. Selling is about being confident about what you have to offer. Selling is about making people confident in making a decision to buy in your presence.

When people want something badly enough, they find a way to afford it. Most people think selling is about selling. But the reality is that selling is about mastering **how people buy**. Take this example.

A young dad walks into a store where musical instruments are sold. An experienced salesperson notices him and asks him, "What musical instrument is your kid learning?"

That one question has already done the job. It is only in rare cases that the young dad won't buy something. People love to buy but hate to be sold.

This is why you need to learn how to sell if you don't already know. All the rich people I know can sell. It seems to be the only thing they have in common (aside from money).

The rich don't work for money. Instead, they see the big picture and position themselves for it. The question you should ask yourself if you have yet to be where you want is this:

What is the big picture here? And how can I have a chunk of that?

# CHAPTER 7: THINK LIKE A MILLIONAIRE AND YOU WILL BECOME ONE

How many millionaires are you friends with? You are the average of the 5 people you spend the most time with. If you want to be wealthier, make new friends that are where you want to be.

◆ ◆ ◆

Lately, I have taken it upon myself to study rich and successful people. I have done all that before, but this time I want to participate in the knowledge and learn afresh. And I keep discovering patterns of success.

For some readers, what you will get from this is not new information. But you have been stuck because you haven't applied that knowledge. The patterns that work for each person differ based on several factors. But if you find something that has great potential to work for you, don't procrastinate.

You can't say it does work for you if you have not tried. Try first before you argue. So, let us begin with the great secret.

## The Big Secret Is Doing Business With Other Millionaires

This is the key. Most speakers talk about making a million by affecting a million lives. But that is often far-fetched for the average person who is still aspiring. This is what drives a lot of people to make products and services.

It is certainly possible to become a millionaire by making a product or service. But the chances are very slim, especially if it is a startup and it is your first time. That is the wrong road. You don't need a product or service. You will eventually, but that is not what you start with.

People glorify ideas. They tell you that one little idea can change the world. They talk about the story of Facebook and the other big success stories. But if Mark Zuckerberg was based in Sri Lanka, do you think he would have become the Facebook CEO that he is today? Think about it.

Your success is influenced by external factors more than you think.

The fastest way to be rich, disregarding your background, is to do business with other millionaires. When you have gotten into their circle and done business with them, then your ideas will matter. Only then will your ideas be met with the support they need to rise to the top. They could without your entering the business circles of millionaires, but the chances are just way better.

Think about doing business with other millionaires.

## Business Is Not Static

Business is not static. Many would consider Apple to be a successful company. But they are still in the ring. They need to work every day to make sure that they remain successful. They make more phones, computers, and gadgets. The story of their success is history. They have to keep fighting like every other person to maintain that success.

Business is not static. There is no such thing as once successful, forever successful. You have to keep the pace up to maintain success. After all the awards and recognition, you still have to get to work the next day.

This is just to tell you that those you consider successful are not living in an unattainable world. You can get into their world. In the same way that you are looking for an edge into success, they are also looking for an edge to further their success and to keep the success they have.

You can influence tomorrow's world of business.

## You Have to See Yourself There

People often think very wrongly about success. They believe they have to do something to get there. They believe they have to be successful before they feel successful. But if you think that way, even if you become successful, the feeling will still elude you.

You need to see yourself successful now. The media has painted some people as superhumans because of their success. The question is:

Do you see yourself as one of those superhumans?

Or do you think they are way above your league? As long as you think they are way above your league, success will elude you. In fact, you will be pushing it away unconsciously. You need to see yourself on the same level as the superstars you adore.

You need to see yourself as rich and successful today. The money part will catch up.

## Go Where Rich People Chill

I read a great book about real estate some years ago. I will never forget the very first piece of advice in the first chapter: to buy property where the rich love to play. How smart!

The key here is to break out of your comfort zone. The new millionaire friends you want to make will not come to your house to meet you. You have to go into their world. You have to get into their environment.

One of the best ways I have discovered for getting into the environment of the rich is to go where they like to relax and enjoy themselves. Now, this doesn't mean you have to take part in whatever they do that you do not approve of. Go to where there is a high likelihood that they will meet you. Remember, **you are in their league**.

It could be a restaurant, bar, park, resort, etc. If it is somewhere you do not approve of, don't go. But if you have nothing personally against the place, you should go. If you currently frequent a cheaper place, consider upgrading.

Go where millionaires chill and make yourself comfortable in that new environment.


## Talk to Strangers

You need to remember that the rich people you will meet don't know who you are. So they will perceive you as you present yourself. But if you go into fan mode when you meet any successful person, it will make the relationship awkward from the start. You will have put yourself beneath them.

This doesn't mean you should be rude or proud. Just be yourself and think of them as the regular people you see every day. Even if you instantly recognize them because of how popular they are, keep your calm and let them introduce themselves.

Talking to strangers is a very important factor in success. And this is not in isolation from the other points above. For this strategy, you talk to strangers where rich people chill. Don't target anybody. Just go with the flow.

Talk to strangers in millionaire environments.

## Change Your World and Your Life Will Change

Many people are waiting for their life to change before they change their world. It really doesn't work that way. You must change your world first. Nobody is saying you should sack your old friends. I am just saying you need new ones.

I don't know about you, but I need more rich friends. This is so you get accustomed to spending time with the rich. If you are uncomfortable around people who are way richer than you, you will have a big problem creating wealth for yourself.

Before you make any product or service, make yourself comfortable around wealth. Change your world first.


## Do This Often

You need to do this until you get used to it. You need to do this until you become uncomfortable where you used to be comfortable. Associations you previously enjoyed that do not encourage your new self-image should become ones you cannot tolerate. Make an environment of wealth your new place of comfort. It will open new pathways in your mind.

The first few times you will do this will feel odd. But the secret is to keep doing it until an environment of wealth becomes your new comfort zone and you can interact with millionaires like you are one of them, even when you have yet to make your own millions.

◆ ◆ ◆

This is a simple pattern of success that works. The question now is:

Will you try it?

This is the plan of action that I have committed myself to. You should try it for 90 days (at least) before you say it doesn't work.

# CHAPTER 8: 7 HABITS THAT CAN HINDER YOU FROM GETTING RICH

A young engineer got two job offers. One offered him $15K monthly plus other benefits. Another company offered him $50K monthly with the same benefits. He chose the $15K offer. Then the $50K company called him to ask why he turned down their offer. The engineer said he thought the $50K offer was a fraud.

Our thinking is shaped by our childhood more than anything. And we take some of these thinking habits into adulthood. Those habits stand in the way of us becoming wealthy. We sabotage ourselves when we are on the verge of a breakthrough. And sometimes we can't even admit it to ourselves that we are uncomfortable with the position we want to advance to.

There are lots of challenges associated with getting rich if you are not raised in a wealthy family. And most of them are mindset-based. In fact, they are mostly unconscious habits.

These are 7 of them that I find most common. Those who got rich found a way to get rid of them.

## 1. Resenting Wealthy People

This is very common. I have never seen anyone become wealthy who resents wealthy people. It is impossible. It is a contradiction. If they accidentally become wealthy, they will shoot themselves in the foot to go back down to where they were. Wealth is not a place for them.

Even if some wealthy people are tyrants, frauds, and immoral people, resenting them isn't okay. To be clear, you resent them because of their display of wealth. You can convince yourself all you want about your stand. But if another person who you know nothing about how they got rich appeared to be flaunting their riches, you would automatically resent them.

If you resent wealthy people, then you resent wealth. That is because you would not have resented them if they didn't look rich. If they showed up looking like an average person on the street, you wouldn't give them any special attention. Nothing would keep you from talking to them any way you like. The only reason you resent them is their display of money. So, it is not people you resent, it is money.

So, if you resent money, how can you have a lot of it?

When I see people drive luxury cars past me, I can't wipe the smile off my face. I love the way they look, I love the way they sound. This is not a "natural" thing. I trained myself to love it.

If objects of luxury trigger resentment in you, you are doing yourself a disservice. Your resentment won't reduce what the other person has. And it is not making society better in any way.

## 2. Telling Your Broke Story

This is very common. Too many people are busy telling their friends stories of when they were broke. The issue is that the more you tell these stories, the more of them you will experience.

People are fond of telling stories of when they had no money. Occasionally, it can be helpful or entertaining to the audience. But if these types of stories are a regular occurrence, you are only creating a broke future for yourself.

Aside from that, everybody will have a mental picture of you as broke. This leads to your having an identity that pushes away money. Let me show you how.

Assume you have a lot of money and there is this guy (among your friends) who is always talking about how broke he is. Suppose that the guy comes to talk to you about a deal or comes to ask you for a loan. Will you give such a person the money? Of course not!

Why? You know what is going to happen afterward. He has said it countless times. You can almost imagine him saying it again. It is the story of his misfortune and how broke he is (again).

If you are having financial issues, don't let others know. Look good, build your confidence, and go make an offer for money! Don't allow people to pity your condition. It is not a good thing.

Money has a way of avoiding people who talk about how broke they are all the time.

### 3. Spending Too Much Time With Broke Friends

Everybody has broke friends. Even the billionaires you know have had them at one point. If you are not careful, they will drag you down to where they are.

It is said that the jokes of the rich are offensive to the poor. Likewise, the jokes of the poor aren't funny to the rich. You can only tolerate broke friends to an extent. After some time, the relationship becomes toxic.

Broke friends are often the ones who go back to childhood or school. They are people that one circumstance or another brought you together with. Sometimes, they are nice people. But if they have a negative attitude toward wealth and riches, it will affect your attempt at growing rich.

If your best friend has a negative attitude to wealth and riches, then it means you will ultimately have to choose between the friendship and growing wealthy.

Sometimes, your friend is not aiming to be wealthy or rich like you. Maybe they have a different calling or passion. But if they fully support your dreams and ambition, that is a friend worth keeping. It is the broke one who is always trying to drag you down that you should walk away from.

It is said that you are the average of 5 people you spend time with. The top 5 people you spend time with highlights where your financial life is going in the short-term.

## 4. Toning Down or Hiding Your Good Fortune

Do you have to hide it if you make a lot of money? Do you have to pretend like you earn 50% less than what you earn? Do you have to dance privately when you get a big financial break?

It is important that you feel happy when you get a good break. Otherwise, you are essentially telling yourself that it isn't really a delightful thing. Money makes people happy. But some just suppress it all the time. But celebrating your good fortune makes way for more.

There are things you don't make a big fuss about. But then there are things you do make a big fuss about. Celebrate yourself. If you are active on social media, showcase your progress in a way that expresses gratitude.

*What about haters?* Well, if you plan to be wealthy, you will inevitably have them. But you will also make some fans and supporters. When you announce yourself like this, your world will tend to produce for you more of what makes you happy.

## 5. Saying, "I Can't Afford It"

If I ask you, "Would you like a Rolls Royce?" what will your answer be? No? Yes? Think about your answer before going forward.

For most people, it is: "I can't afford it." The interesting thing is that I said nothing about buying a Rolls Royce. I just asked if you would like one. You may still be thinking, "Well, I don't like the car, I prefer a Benz." But if I offered to give you one as a gift, would you turn it down? I bet you wouldn't.

Or would you be afraid even to receive it? For those who agonize over the taxes or maintenance of the car, your problem is your narrow frame. The poor mindset still controls you. Let me show you how to overcome that.

If I were to receive a Rolls Royce like that and I couldn't afford to maintain it, I would instantly register a company. Start leasing the car for people who need it for special events. By doing that, I would turn it into an asset. Plus, I could rent it from myself from time to time. You see?

The things we say not only affect the world around us, but affect ourselves as well. There are things you have prevented your mind from thinking about based on your response or reaction.

When you say, "I can't afford it," it's like the program shuts down in your brain. Thoughts are things. If you want something in your life, the first place you need to create it is in your thoughts. Many go against themselves even in their own minds through their defeatist words.

When you say something like "I can't afford it," your mind records that thing as something you are not able to have. Your mind just takes that notion as an eternal fact that isn't subject to change. "I can't afford it" means you will always be in a position where you can't afford it. Thoughts are timeless.

But if you say something really good about your state (that you believe), even if it is not true at the moment, your mind gradually adjusts your reality until it becomes true. It may take some years, but it happens eventually.

Instead of saying, "I can't afford it," why don't you open up your mind to possibilities by asking the question: "How can I afford it?" There is always a "how" if you look hard enough.

If you like it and you find it desirable, don't push it away. Always use your words to bring good things closer to you.

## 6. Smart Excuses

When given a challenge, some people start making excuses even before they begin. Excuses lie in the opposite direction of success. Success produces riches and wealth. Excuses produce failure.

Success has stories, failure has excuses.

The most interesting part is that the story of success begins before taking the first step. Excuses for failure begin before taking the first step. Based on a person's initial response, you can tell where it is all going to end.

A governor held a meeting and invited the top professors and academicians in his state. He wanted to create a new university in the state. But he had the idea to space out the campus over several towns, a multi-campus system. All the professors opposed it. They believed it wouldn't work. But one professor spoke differently and said he had seen a place where such has worked before. That was how the professor got the job of heading the new state university.

Do you have the habit of stating the various ways something won't work? Or are you someone who talks about the ways it could work? Eliminating the chances of failure is good. But if you are not careful, you will become so focused on failure that you produce failure for yourself.

Money likes the person who gets things done—especially the person who shuts up and gets it done. Such people are quickly promoted, and they get offered bigger and better opportunities.

Wealthy people who fought their way out of poverty first had to kill this habit of excuses (and complaints).

## 7. Asking for Free Stuff

From childhood, people from wealthy families are raised to use the expensive stuff. Most other families train their younger ones to go for the cheap version and to embrace that which is free.

Free things are bad. They are bad because they condition you to a state where you lose the actual value of something. There is nothing really free in this world. Everything has value. Even handshakes and hugs have value (but are not monetized).

If you get a product or service for free, it is because someone paid for it. The product or service cost someone time, skill, expertise, energy, and so on. To enjoy it without having a feel of the cost is dangerous to a person's mindset.

First, if you love free things, the best things in life will elude you. And this is not just about the expensive things in life. It also includes valuable things that are not monetized. A good example is new, productive people who can help you get to your next level.

Second, if you love free things, you will extend that thought to other aspects of your life. For example, you will attach little or no value to your time. If you don't value your time, you are unlikely to value the time of other people.

Money is the primary way we measure value in this world. Whenever you enjoy something for free, always try to reciprocate for it with something valuable. This is not about trying to pay for everything, sometimes it is just about giving sincere gratitude. Gratitude has value.

People who ask for free stuff never show gratitude. They place little or no value on everything, including themselves. This is why the good things of life always like to dodge them.

These are very common habits today. I bet a few people came to your mind as you were reading. And perhaps you even saw a bit of your current state in some points. You can choose to fight this information and defend yourself for your thought process. Or you can choose to say YES to a life of wealth.

# CHAPTER 9: 7 WAYS THE RICH THINK DIFFERENTLY ABOUT MONEY

The rich think differently about money. Regular people think about the things money can buy whenever the subject of money comes up. This is why they are often alarmed at how much money the ultra-rich have.

Regular people will often think about the wealth of the rich in terms of, "What can they buy with that amount of money?" But that question is part of the reasons why such a wealthy status is unattainable for them.

When rich people see money, they don't see things. If you wish to join the club of the rich, you have to stop seeing money in terms of what it can buy.

The rich see money as a remote control. The rich see money as power. The rich see money as a tool. This is why they have billions and still stay in the game. Meanwhile, the average person would retire and go on vacation for the rest of their life with $30 million.

A rich person in this context is a person with the capacity to make at least $1 million in the span of a year even if they lose everything today.

You know those kinds of people. When Steve Jobs was kicked out of Apple, the company he co-founded, it was easy for him to bounce back with another company (Pixar). Getting the money he needed to start over was pretty easy. He already had a reputation for being an innovator.

How do you think Steve looked at money? Or maybe Warren Buffett, who still lives in the same house he has lived in for over 30 years. Warren lives such a modest lifestyle, it makes you wonder why someone like him holds on to billions. It is because he sees money differently.

The rich don't see money in terms of what money can buy.

Here are 7 ways the rich see money differently:

## 1. The Rich See Money as People

When regular people think about money, they think of what to sell to get it. But the rich focus on those who have the money. In their eyes, money represents people.

Think about it; all the money in the world is under the custody of someone. If you can get a person to open their hands, you get what they have. The average mind targets the money in people's hands. The rich target the people. This is because they know that if they win the people, they get the money.

In the eyes of the rich, bags of money walk past them on the street every day. They don't see people as money. But they see money as people.

## 2. The Rich See Money as a Complement (and not Competitor) to Time

The average mind that goes through school thinks of money as a reward for work and time spent. The rich don't. This is why the rich don't look for where to earn money in exchange for time. The rich would rather look for where to ask for money and get it.

Money complements time. Money makes time enjoyable. However, truly rich people would never trade their time for money. They use their time to pursue their dreams and do work that gives them fulfillment.

The regular person tries to find fulfillment in the trade of time for money. And it is a struggle. This is why rich people can work 20 hours a day and not complain. They didn't choose what they do because of the promise of financial compensation for their time.

## 3. The Rich Don't Feel Cheated When People Take Advantage of Them Financially

This is an attitude towards money that is very difficult for regular people. Rich people easily overlook it when other people take advantage of them. Not that they don't take notice, but they often take a relaxed stance because they will likely use that to gain a favor in the future.

Many times those who take advantage of the generosity of the rich do not respond in kind when the tables turn. This eventually destroys the relationship. And the rich use that to eliminate unprofitable ties.

The rich won't argue with you when you cheat them. But if you do not come through for them when most needed, you can say goodbye to the advantages of their acquaintance. They see money as a tool, and hence are not emotionally connected to it to the extent of screaming at someone trying to pocket some change.

## 4. The Rich See Money as What It Is Going to Produce

If you owe a rich man $1 million, he won't be mad because of the $1 million. Instead, he will be mad because of what that $1 million would have turned into if he had it.

Rich people are always looking at the future value of what they currently have. The present value is only useful when there is an immediate purchase to be made. What really matters to the rich is what the value of their money will look like in the future.

## 5. The Rich See Money as a Tool to Shape Their Personas

To the rich, persona is reality. A lot of rich people take the way others perceive them seriously. Persona is how people perceive you. Regular people often rely on the natural course of life to create their persona, but rich people are often proactive about this.

Using money to build a persona is not limited to expensive outfits, expensive parties, and the like. In fact, some rich people live very modest lives. However, they make the necessary noise with their charities, donations, and achievement reports to garner public attention.

Rich people work extra hard in this area in order to be loved by regular people. This is because being neutral will create problems when there is an issue of bad press. If they don't work hard to create a good perception of themselves, someone might wake up one morning and paint them in the worst possible light. And they can lose a lot of good fortune and wealth before they have the chance to set the record straight.

To the rich, money is a tool to shape their public persona.

## 6. The Rich See Money as the True Expression of People's Interest

Here is an interesting way to test public interest on any product (or service) you are working on. Show it to people. Ask if they like it. Then ask if they will be willing to pay 10x what you intend to charge for it.

Of course, the answer will likely be a NO, but watch out for how they tell you the NO. Those that suggest (without being prompted) an amount they can pay for the solution are those who are really interested in the solution.

An interest that is not coupled with money is not a real interest. It is just a mere wish. When people are willing to trade their hard-earned cash for something, that is the true test of interest. Rich people have mastered this.

## 7. The Rich See Money as an Effective Tool to Buy Other People's Time

The rich make more time for themselves by buying time from other people willing to trade it. This is not a bad thing on either end. It is just a matter of need. The rich have money but need time. And there will always be someone who has time and needs money.

Money is a great tool to bring time and talent to your camp. There are lots of people in the world who wouldn't be working on what they are working on if they were not being paid. Money is very useful in buying time and talent.

There are other ways the rich see money, but I think these are enough to get you thinking in the right direction.

# CHAPTER 10: HOW THE LAW OF ATTRACTION WORKS FOR MONEY

You can't really attract money. Money doesn't work that way. Money is something used to get things.

Money is not material itself. The substances used for money have changed over the years. Today we use paper money, and it varies from one country to another. In fact, there are differences in the currencies of each country.

Presently, a lot of countries are even encouraging electronic cash. The banking system is creating all kinds of cards for people. So in actuality a large portion of the money being used is not really tangible.

We want money because of what money can buy. I don't think there is anyone who wants to store cash in their house just for the sake of having it.

So, money is a vehicle that gets you what you want. *Does this mean that you have to attract the end goal itself and not money?* Not exactly. There is a way, but it is not as direct as attracting other things.

But first, let's understand how the law of attraction really works.

## The Real Law of Attraction

The law of attraction became popular in 2006 when the movie (and book) *The Secret* were released. The message was so attractively delivered that it sent many people into a frenzy despite not actually understanding it.

Some mocked the concept, saying that you cannot possibly get what you want by daydreaming about it. And they were right. Daydreaming definitely won't work.

The law of attraction is a law, like the law of gravity. The law of gravity pulls every object on earth to its center. This is why if you throw any object up, it will come down.

The law of gravity works whether you like it or not. The law of gravity doesn't care about your feelings or what you want. It was not created by any human—we only discovered it. It was already in effect, long before any of us was born.

It is the same with the law of attraction. It works regardless of what you think about it. It is working right now whether you agree with it or not. It doesn't care about your feelings.

The law of attraction pulls what you desire towards you as long as some conditions are met. (You will learn those conditions soon.) It is like when you make up your mind to buy a particular type of car, and when you go out all you see on the road is that particular type of car.

Some people say the cars were always there and you only just began to notice it. While that is true, there is also a combined effect of attraction. Now that you are thinking of that particular car, the law of attraction will bring it into your world.

The human being is a magnet. The world was designed for humans, not vice versa. Everything in the world is like metal to the human magnet. Most people do not understand or take advantage of this, and hence they keep attracting what they don't want into their lives.

Whether you like it or not, you are a walking magnet. Your internal magnet is programmed naturally by the environment you grew up in. This is why many people make the same life choices as their parents or friends or relatives or someone they look up to.

The concept in the movie *The Secret* is that you can reprogram your magnet. Most people have been programmed from birth to attract the wrong things. Some attract good things but not what they actually want.

This is the real deal about the law of attraction. But for it to work for you, there is something you should know.

## You Cannot Attract What You Are Not on the Same Level of Vibration With

This part of the understanding is thanks to Bob Proctor, who made an appearance in the movie *The Secret*. He is a prosperity teacher who has been teaching about the abundance mindset for over 58 years.

He gave a brilliant explanation that counters all those who mock the law of attraction. And the explanation is this:

You cannot attract what you are not on the same level of vibration with.

He explains a principle known as the law of vibration. The law of attraction is actually a subset of the law of vibration. The law of vibration simply states that everything is in motion. It means everything vibrates at its own frequency.

You may think some things are totally still, but there is nothing still in the universe. Everything is moving.

Attraction only happens between two entities that are vibrating on the same frequency. The human being as a magnet is capable of changing frequencies. Unless you are on the same frequency as what you want to attract, you won't be able to attract what you want.

## The Mind and Pictures

Attraction is done with the mind. It is important to have a clear mental picture of what you desire. Then, you visualize it.

Another mistake people make is to visualize something that would be a violation of another person, the environment, or the world. An example is desiring a particular item that belongs to another person.

Desiring something like what another person has is good. But when the thing itself belongs to another person, then wishing to own it yourself is a violation.

Using the law of attraction is not about sitting down to idly daydream. Instead, it is a running picture in the mind, by which you experience what you desire in your mind.

The mind cannot really tell the difference between a real experience and an imagined experience. The goal is to give your mind an experience you want to have, as though you have already had it. If you make it happen many times in your mind, it won't be long before it happens for real.

The law of attraction is creating an experience you want to have, so that your mind has a record of it and produces more of the real situation for you.

Sometimes it takes sitting down "idly" to visualize. But remember that you cannot attract what you are not on the same level with.

## Money and Goals

What does it mean to be on the same level of vibration with what you want? It is a simple question. Do you look like the recipient of what you want?

Let's assume you want to make $3M yearly from your business, and you currently make $150K. Study a particular business in your industry making $3M. Study them well.

If you hear on the news that a company like yours is making $3M per year, would you believe it? The answer is "no" most times. The task now is to make your company look like a company that makes $3M per year. This is what it means to get on the frequency of your goals.

Your goals cannot be up there while you are down here. You won't attract your goals into your environment. Instead, you have to get into the environment where your goals are.

This is how the law of attraction works.

## Know What You Actually Want

It is hard (if not impossible) to attract what you are not specific about. The human magnet only works with specificity. If you are not specific about what you want, you will get something you don't want but were more specific about.

The human magnet is not sophisticated. It cannot really tell the difference between what you desire and what you don't. Rather, it will bring to you what you obsess about and the experiences you keep replaying in your mind.

This is why some get angry at the law of attraction. They only get the things they don't want. This is because they spend time visualizing what they don't want rather than what they do want.

Also, if your mind is confused and yet to be made up, it is difficult to attract anything. Your mind has to be made up first before the law can begin to work for you.

Imagination and visualization are not all there is to the law of attraction. Remember, the idea is to fool your mind into thinking that what you want has already happened. So simply visualizing where you want to be while you are where you are is not enough. Sometimes you have to smell the leather.

If what you want is a car, for example, go to the dealer's place. Sit inside the car. Take it for a spin (if they allow you). Soak yourself in the experience of owning it. If it is a house, go to the house and check it out. As you walk through every room, imagine yourself living in it.

Your visualization must be recorded as an experience in your mind. You want it to be more of a memory than a daydream.

## Attracting Money

Now that you understand how the law of attraction works for other things, you should be able to guess how it works for money.

There are two major ways it works. The first is wealth triggers. Money attracts money. You have to bring things into your environment that remind you that you are wealthy. This is so that the image will keep running in the background of your thoughts.

Some people buy works of art. Some buy clothing and accessories. It just has to be something expensive in your environment that connects you to where you want to go.

You need to have something real that your mind will use as a basis to connect you to where you want to be.

The second way to work the law of attraction is through words. The law of attraction often fails for people because they negate what they want to attract with their words. They use their words to push what they want away from them.

You cannot imagine what you want, negate it with your speech, and still expect it to come to pass. Your words must align with what you desire.

When it comes to money, your desire must be apparent in every conversation, especially in friendly conversations. You must say it and keep saying it. And when the opportunity arises, you must ask for it boldly.

People will be hesitant to give you a sum of money that you cannot mention with a neutral expression. If you give a greedy smile when you mention the amount, you still need to practice while you visualize.

Money responds to words.

## Act Like You Have It

This is different from the saying "fake it to make it." With "fake it to make it," you are pretending to have something that you don't. In "act like you have it," you know well that you are of the type of person that has what you desire.

If you have not gotten on the frequency of where you want to be, it is difficult to portray this confidence, and can strike others as false. But when you are on the same level as your goals, you know you are "it" even without having it.

Remember that there are people who have money and still are not in that state of mind. Getting into the state really has nothing to do with having. But once you are there, it becomes easy to have anything on that level that you want.

This is also useful when it comes to visualization. You practice who you want to become. If you want to be a millionaire startup founder, assume you are one and imagine you are being interviewed in your mind. Then try to answer those interview questions like it is a real event happening. (This is only for yourself, though, and not for anyone else.)

The wonderful thing about an exercise like this is that it brings clarity. You can gain insights about the next step you ought to take towards your goal.

This is how the law of attraction works for money.

## A Reminder

You must remember that the law can work against you just as it can work for you. If you do not actively put the law to work, it is still working nevertheless. It may only be weak magnetically, and it will keep attracting what you don't want.

The law of attraction can bring you anything if properly applied. If you are not getting the results you want, read this again and see what you are missing.

# PART III: HOW TO GET STARTED

"So we got it for $126M."

"How?"

"The bank paid, our partners signed, but we get to use it!"

# CHAPTER 11: GETTING STARTED
# WITHOUT MONEY

Two hours per day can increase your income 10x in a year.

Many times we think that getting rich is all about playing the money game. Yes, it is. But if you start the money game too early you might harm your potential. Here is what I mean.

The games you can play with $20M will probably ruin your finances if you try them with $20K. You must know the money game and how to play it. But at the initial stages, you have to first rise up financially.

Rising up financially is not a difficult task. But it becomes frustrating when you expect the magic to happen overnight. Magic does happen overnight when playing with big money. But when you are just rising, it takes time.

Of course, everybody has 24 hours in a day, but many people make time their enemy. 2 hours every day for a year is 730 hours. 730 hours dedicated to one task is enough to make you better than 99% of people who practice the same craft.

The benefits won't come overnight, but when they do come, it will be a windfall. That early momentum is important. Don't joke with it.

## To Get Started, You Don't Need Money

You don't need money to get started. In fact, the money you have when you are getting started is a big problem. This is because you will keep looking at that money like it is a ticket. And it is not. In fact, you will probably lose all of it.

I have discovered that people's survival instinct is incredibly strong. As long as you are not battling for financial survival, you will naturally be complacent. But the moment you are battling for financial survival, your mind opens up.

This is why it is easier for someone who is $50M in debt to get rich than someone who has $10K. Someone who has $10K is very likely comfortable. But the person $50M in debt has to either make millions or drown. It is a much scarier place, but the drive to become a multimillionaire is there.

We instinctively want to avoid that scary place. But there is no motivation like a scary place. If you need the money badly enough, you will find a way to get it.

But you don't need money to get started. There is a better way. It is better to create an income stream that can absorb any shock of early failure.

And it is by using time to create a steady flow of substantial income.

## Set a Goal

Many people's problem starts with the fact that they don't have a goal. Of course, many would say they have a goal, but when they lay it down, it turns out to be a passive wish.

A wish is something you hope to achieve in the future. A goal is something definite you want to achieve that has a deadline. A goal without a date is a wish.

When you set a target for yourself and put a deadline to it, that is a goal. Then you can go one step further and start telling your friends that you will achieve that target at that time. That will put you on the edge.

The kind of goal you set, in this case, is a goal for mastery. You have to pick a lucrative skill to master. The skill must be connected to what you eventually wish to become in the long-term.

Set a goal to master a skill. The best way to get started on the road to riches is to become a master and an expert in something there is a high and lucrative demand for.

Pick one thing to become an expert on.

## Every Little Thing Compounds Over Time

A friend sent me a book last year that explains this well, entitled *The Compound Effect*. The message of the book is that success is the sum total of little things compounded over time. I have found this to be true.

When you set a target of what you want to become good at and you add a deadline, then you dedicate time every day towards it. Two hours every day might look small, but that is 730 hours a year. And 3,650 hours in 5 years.

Let's now say you dedicate 4 hours every day to your target. That is 1,460 hours in a year. And 7,300 in 5 years.

If you think 5 years is a long time, let me remind you that 2015 is now 5 years ago. And if you are reading this in any other year that is not 2020, just count 5 years backward.

What were you doing in 2015? Believe me, that question hits me too. If you had dedicated 4 hours every day from 2015, you would be a pro by now. This is called the compound effect.

When you get started, the first 60 days will probably be the hardest. After this, your brain will accept it as a routine. You might feel you are not improving during this time, but you really are.

The compound effect is a geometric growth sequence. It is like the penny doubled every day for 31 days. On day 3, you look like the biggest fool in the world. But on day 31, you are the envy of the world.

Just in case you have never heard this before, if you are asked to choose between a million dollars and a penny that doubles every day for 31 days, pick the penny that doubles. Do the math.

## Why 99% of the World's Population Live on 1% of the World's Money

Someone once pointed out that if everyone in the world was given the same amount of money and life was allowed to go on, it wouldn't be long before the top 1% control 99% of the money again.

Many complain that the system is rigged in favor of the rich. Yes, that is true. But the way I see it, why not join them? Those complaining want to be rich by staying poor. And that is against the natural order.

If you are an expert on something that the world has a high demand for, you have the potential to be rich. Being rich begins with having something valuable to offer the world.

99% of the world have not mastered anything. And that is the starting point. If they have mastered anything, it is something that keeps them as someone else's employee.

If you want to join the exclusive class of the rich, first become an expert in something there is a high demand for. With as little as 2 hours a day, you can get started. And as you get better, dedicate more time to it.

And then you hit the magic 10,000 hours before you know it.

## The Magic of 10,000 Hours

The best book about success I have read thus far is *Outliers* by

Malcolm Gladwell. If you have not read this book, I highly recommend it.

*Outliers* introduces this concept of 10,000 hours. The idea is that it takes 10,000 hours of practice to become a pro at anything. And not just 10,000 scattered hours; it has to be 10,000 consistent hours, built up one day after another.

If we follow this magic number, it will take roughly 14 years to be a pro at something you practice 2 hours every day. Meanwhile, if you "up your game" to 4 hours a day, it will take you roughly 7 years. What if you can do it for 6 hours every day? That is 4 years and 6 months!

Okay, let's get realistic.

## The Compound Effect + Magic

We all know you can't start with 6 hours every day. You will probably get worn out and discouraged before the end of the week. So let's assume you start with 2 hours every day and double it every 60 days. And, of course, we cap it at 12 hours (instead of 16 hours) per day.

Hmmm. How long will it take you to get to the magic 10,000? Take a guess.

It will take you 2 years and 6 months. That is less than 3 years. Think about it.

You could be introduced to some stage as a leading world expert in "something" in 3 years.

Okay. Maybe the idea of doubling is too high for you. What about 2 hours every day, where you add an extra 2 hours every 30 days. And cap it off at 8 hours per day. That seems easy enough.

How long to the magic 10,000? Take a guess.

It will take you 3 years and 6 months. Less than 4 years. How about that for realistic?

## The Added-Cushion Effect

This is just a made-up phrase by me. But after I'm through explaining it, you will see that it makes so much sense.

When you start practicing a new skill for 2 hours a day, it will seem like the hardest thing in the world. Many times you will cringe and wish the 2 hours were over. But after 30 days, it becomes your routine.

At some point closer to the 30-day mark, you will start to actually enjoy it. And this is caused by one of two reasons. The first is that you are getting to see the results and you love what you see.

It is like when you start working out and lifting weights. The first few days are hard. But the moment you start seeing those muscles and abs when you look in the mirror, you are pumped up with excitement to do more.

The second reason is that the process itself is becoming enjoyable because your skills are improving.

This is like when you're finally able to lift the weight you saw the biggest guy lifting the first time you walked into the gym. It is a really good feeling. But you'll never experience it if you don't endure the first set of days.

Of course, the hard periods will come again. The days of zero motivation. All you need is to stick to your schedule. No more, no less.

The added-cushion effect is when it starts to feel good. That is when you see yourself doing it for 6 hours when you had scheduled just 4 hours. You start discussing it with friends, then someone recommends you somewhere. And then you get a deal to focus on it full time. It suddenly becomes something you can spend 8 hours doing comfortably.

Some days you can go as far as 12 hours. And suddenly you get a breakthrough that puts you at the forefront in the field globally.

The added-cushion effect only comes into play when you take the compound effect seriously.

## Make Time Your Friend

The ironic thing about all of this is that it works inversely too. Meaning that when you spend time doing things that add no value to your future, it will get compounded too.

This is why people grow old and go broke. The many years of complacency finally added up.

If you question most rich people, the lifestyle that brought them to where they are is boring and oftentimes difficult. But they stuck to it for years. That is why it works and why it is still working.

The things you do repeatedly matters. Make time work for you and not against you. For example, the years will come and go whether you like it or not. But whether you will be an expert in 5 years' time depends on what you do every day from today.

You don't need money to begin your journey to get rich. You have time. Use the time instead.

# CHAPTER 12: THE BEST "GET-RICH" STARTING POINT FOR PEOPLE NOT BORN INTO A WEALTHY FAMILY

**M**oney attracts money. You do know that, right? That is why people born into wealthy families have a headstart in getting rich. It takes most of them very minimal effort. Most of what they have to do already seems natural to them.

I recently had a conversation with a friend. He just started working about a year ago. He has begun to see the way life is and how the school system and the religious culture has totally deceived everybody.

He initially had the choice to either stay in the small town where he grew up or move to the nearby big city. I advised him to move. Interestingly, he had been offered a good salary and convenient commute to stay in the town. When he moved to the big city, he got a similar offer (in a different job). But the offer became small because of the expenses of living in the big city.

Of course, he chose the big city, and not because of city life.

Rather, he took my advice to widen his scope. When we met up to talk, he had so much to say. His perspective of "rich" has changed. Now, he is hungry for some real success.

As our discussion grew specific, he asked me:

"What can someone like me do to get to the top because I don't have the money to get started?"

Before this, he talked about how he had two kinds of friends growing up. There were those who came from a rich family and those who didn't. And from a young age, he noticed that those from rich families became friends with each other and not with the other group.

He was able to make friends with the rich kids because he was academically high-achieving. But his average friends kept holding him back. He noticed that to make friends with the rich kids, you must act as if you come from a rich family.

As it was then, so it is in the grownup world. Or rather, you act rich to get rich. Practice being rich to actually become rich. This led to my friend's question: what about those who just don't have?

There are many things that hold people back from their dreams. No one dreams of a life of suffering, being a beggar, or barely getting by. Everyone dreams of success, even though some may find it hard to admit. The reason is not just that they don't know where to start, but they have also allowed negative notions about money to take root in their minds.

## Money Is Not the Root of All Evil

Is money the root of all evil? Many people erroneously believe it is. They may not admit it, but it is a truth they hold dear to their heart.

This notion was supposedly taken from the Bible. However, it is a misquote.

What the Bible says is:

"The love of money is the root of all evil."

It is not about money. Money is an inanimate object. Money cannot love itself. Love of money is a human characteristic. Another word for this is avarice.

*How is the love of money the root of all evil?* Good question. Money is a tool. We desire money because of the things money can do. It is not wrong or bad to desire money for the things money can do. However, when a person desires money just to have more of it, then it becomes dangerous.

Someone who has the "love of money" syndrome does not care if they lose their soul in the quest for money. In fact, they willingly sell their souls for money. There are those who do this out of desperation. And there are those who do this out of the desire to be superior.

Many think only rich people can be examples of those who have sold their souls for money. But the reality is that more poor and average people have done that. And when someone has sold their soul for money, evil things don't look evil. They can create elaborate explanations to defend bad actions. This is what is actually the root of all evil.

Your moral compass is eroded when you are already blinded and biased by money. People sometimes make mistakes and bad choices, but those who are blinded by the love of money will defend their wrongdoings in the face of money.

Here is the summary: if someone can make you change your mind about a stance or subject just by offering you money, you do have the "love of money."

It means that if you were offered enough money, you would "accidentally" push someone in front of a moving truck. (This example is figurative but it can also be literal.)

Money is neither good nor evil. Instead, it is people who expose themselves for who they really are with money.

So, when you hear someone try to quote this beside you, make the right adjustments. It is not "money is the root of all evil." Even the more accurate phrase "the love of money is the root of all evil" is quite confusing. I think this is better:

Avarice is the root of all evil.

People will likely ask you what avarice is. Then you can explain to them. Avarice is simply when a large amount of money can make you do something that you normally shouldn't, especially something bad.

Avarice often springs out of lack of money. It also springs from the lack of understanding of how to make money and grow rich.

Why don't you become rich so that you won't be tempted by avarice?

## You Don't Need Money to Make Money

The rich use money to make money. And it is a very effective strategy of success. The moment you make some money, you position yourself to make more. And it works.

The problem is that people who don't have money can't do that. And these are people who are not from wealthy families, who were raised to work for money. Unfortunately, most of them start spending before they start earning and by default are behind perpetually in their finances.

But the good news is that you don't need money to make money. There are different types of currencies in the world. There are financial currencies like the US Dollar and Pound Sterling. And there are also social currencies.

You may not have a lot of financial currencies, but you can use your social currency to get rich.

If you don't have money to start with, you then need to get good at using social currencies. This is something that has dawned on me recently.

## What You Need Is a Plug

The easiest way to be a millionaire is to do deals with other millionaires. But they won't accept you into their circle just because you want to join. You need a legitimate excuse to get in among them. You need a plug.

The stories I have studied of successful people who became rich at a very young age, coming from a disadvantaged background, always have one very interesting element. They all had one older person who was rich, who introduced them into a group of rich people that changed their paradigm.

I call those older rich people "plugs." If you don't have money, what you need is a plug. A plug is someone rich who can bring you into their circle of rich people. This makes up for your lack of money and changes your paradigm.

## Eat From the Table of Elders

Words matter. One of the most effective ways of changing your financial situation is to change the people you have conversations with. Not just money conversations but conversations in general. It changes your entire paradigm when you see the way rich people think about things.

For example, they can start talking about a new government policy. While you may be looking only at what the direct impact will be on people, you will find rich people talking about how consumer choices will change because of the new policy. And they can even stretch the subject into how the flow of money will be affected by that singular policy.

The way you see things gradually becomes different. And you will begin to notice things around you that you didn't before. It is like when you decide the brand of car you want to buy, and all of a sudden you begin to see it everywhere.

It was just like that when I started studying marketing. Instantly, I began to notice the marketing in everything. And I mean everything. I would see a signpost and begin to think about its appeal and how much more effectively that appeal could have been structured.

If you don't have the money to get started, then you need a plug to sit at the table of rich people.

There is an old proverb that says the one who eats from the table of elders has become one of them.

## If You Are the Richest Person in the Room, Find Another Room

Finding another room is not easy. Finding a good plug is hard. But giving up is worse.

Many would rather be a leader among paupers than a servant among kings. And that is the problem of a lot of people. They just don't want to be uncomfortable.

The more uncomfortable you can make yourself, the richer you can actually be.

It is just like my friend, who was comfortable with his average friends and allowed them to pull him away from the rich kids. Now, the rich kids are potential plugs that he cannot access.

The answer I gave to my friend's big question is what I have tried to explain thus far. The way for him to get rich is to put himself in situations where he is the poorest person in attendance. And to do that as often as possible. It is a propelling force.

You don't have to abandon the room where you are the richest. If you have teaching tendencies, like me, you might want to stay there. But you must find a higher room for yourself.

Is this the only way for someone from a not-so-rich background to get wealthy? Far from it. There are definitely other ways. But this one is damn effective.

## Spend Your Time With People Who Talk About Big Deals

If you want to do a deal worth $10 million, start spending time with those who have. If you want to start earning $10K a month, start spending time with people who do.

It is always better when you can physically meet those people and take part in those discussions. But in cases where you can't find that yet, you can get audio lectures and podcasts. Videos are also good. But audios are more powerful.

This is the reason. When you watch a video, your principal sense in action is your sight, even though hearing takes place too. But when you listen to audio, the principal sense is your hearing. The brain often stores information in patterns and pictures. So your mind will create a picture based on those words they are speaking better than when you are watching them actually talk.

Audio involves imagination. Imagination is often greater than sight. But there are some cases where sight is necessary. This is because the mind cannot imagine what it cannot fathom. And it cannot fathom what it has not seen.

The moment you can imagine yourself there, it becomes easy to get there.

But the best of all is if you are physically present at the discussion. Then, all your senses are connected. Your imagination is also involved. This is because your mind stores that event as a memory. So every time you go back to the memory, your mind can bring you details you noticed but you weren't conscious of at the time.

Spending time with people discussing big deals is a way to prepare your mind for success. Then you grow to the point where you start making meaningful contributions to those discussions. And you will soon find yourself doing the deals you were once wishing for.

Anybody can be rich. Even if you come from the poorest of the poor families.

The mistake some people make is that they shoot too high and lose the sense of the words "I can." It's like someone who hasn't seen $100K, who wants to get into the world of people dealing with over $1 billion. It is possible, but it is quite an extreme case.

Start with trying to add one more zero to the money you currently have. Then you can climb step by step to the level of riches you desire.

# CHAPTER 13: 7 STEPS TO BE WORTH 10 TIMES WHAT YOU ARE RIGHT NOW

It is in your power to make 10 times what you currently make. You have to first believe it. If you do not, it will be hard for any of these ideas to work for you. And if you already make 6 figures, it is still possible. You only have to implement these ideas on a larger scale.

I learned a very important lesson through an experience I had last year. I wanted to increase the amount my side income was generating. I thought what I was doing was wrong and that I needed to do something entirely new. And I focused on the new while ignoring the obvious (which was making a little money at that time).

After a while, I discovered I was in the same place with the new gig as I was with the old. I had just made myself busier. There was no meaningful progress. When I realized that, I went back to the old gig (which was writing). Then I focused on it and made a little change, and that made all the difference.

The little change was that I decided to treat it like a day job. I also made some insightful changes to my outlook. I decided to take the work very seriously, like I was reporting to a boss. That was when I stepped on the accelerator. And every day, I make time to work on it.

Since then, I have seen phenomenal growth. In just a few months, my income from writing has grown by more than 10x.

The principles responsible for this growth (and similar growth of other people's income I have seen) is what I hope you gain from this article. You don't have to learn another profession or skill to get you 10x what you earn right now. You can scale the one you know. Here is how:

## 1. Celebrity Endorsement

This is a game-changer. If you have worked for (or with) someone famous, you should use that to improve your image. This could also be a brand or company that is highly recognized. It doesn't have to be a celebrity everybody knows, it could be a fairly big name in your industry or niche.

Brand association is one of the things that gives big clients the confidence to do business with you. Big clients want to know who you have worked for so they can feel comfortable handing you that fat check. So, if there is any means by which you can get yourself and your skills endorsed by a big name—do it.

The impact of this will not be immediate on your income. But when you combine this with other strategies, the effect will be profound.

## 2. Target Players With Money

The #1 problem low-earning people have is cheap clients. In many cases, you don't see how you have designed your outlook and image to attract cheap clients. And cheap clients will always get cheaper in doing business with you.

Some are not cheap by nature, they are just broke. They can't afford your next level. And if you keep working with them, you will always remain where you are. Growth always involves change. And change always takes courage. You must be willing to step out of your comfort zone of cheap clients to start attracting big clients.

Target players with money. Players with money are people who can afford to pay you 10x what you are earning. You may be thinking, "do people like this exist?" Yes, they do. But if you don't target them, you will never see them. It is all about you stepping out of your comfort zone.

Do some industry research and find someone who does something similar to what you do but earns 10x as much. Find out: who does the person cater to? How can you start serving a similar client base?

## 3. Build a Personal Brand of Your New Level

What I mean by a personal brand here is simply your work image. Use a more professional photo. Pick a social media platform and build up your brand there.

I do not believe in having multiple social media accounts, especially at the early stages. Have just one and focus on it. When you have built one to a remarkable extent, then you can branch off into another.

Developing your online visibility is very important. When clients know you before they get in touch with you, they expect you to charge big. In that way, the road to 10x income is already paved.

## 4. Find Your Niche

Generalists don't earn much. In every profession, specialists are always favored over generalists. Think of it this way: if you have a problem with your eye, would you prefer a family doctor to work on it or an eye surgeon?

If you are still unsure of where to specialize, take your time. But know that you have to specialize sooner or later. Don't get caught up in looking for the most lucrative area to specialize in. That is the wrong approach. Instead, think about what area suits you best.

Never be hasty in picking a niche. This is because you will be there for the rest of your professional life. If possible, test different niches. See which one you bond with the most. There are high-paying clients in every niche.

You don't need a lot of high-paying clients to make a lot of money. This is why you should never let the fact that there are lots of high-paying clients in a particular niche get to you. You could have just 2 high-paying clients and be making a 6-figure sum.

## 5. Reject Low-Income Jobs

You ought to let your world know that you have upgraded. This means you need to start rejecting low-income jobs. This might sound counterintuitive, but it is a necessary step. But this is after you have picked a niche and started growing your personal brand.

You need to create a system that can satisfy your low-income clients. You can have a network of people you will refer them to. Or you can create a perpetual system of resources such as blog posts, webinars, etc., where they can receive value from you with little or no cost.

Rejecting low-income jobs will allow you to focus all your attention on the high-paying jobs. And you need that focus to be able to do the things required to draw in high-paying clients.

## 6. Position Yourself as an Expert
## With Substantial Content

Getting high-paying clients is all about positioning. Positioning is all about putting out content. This is on the same line as building your personal brand. Your personal brand has to present you as an expert. This is the goal.

But to get there, you need to produce a lot of content. Don't even bother counting or waste time overthinking. Just get to work and start pumping out content related to your field. The only caveat is that you must be producing high-quality content.

If all you do is smart titles and fluff content, people will soon notice and you will lose the attention you once easily retained. Quality content is of the essence.

## 7. Increase Your Price

When you have implemented a number of these changes, the only thing left is to increase your price. This is the most important of all the changes. No one will pay you at your new level if you still quote your old rates.

If you have made changes and nobody has noticed, the increase in price will make them notice. You don't have to get everything perfectly right before you increase your price. You just do it when the time is right. It may not be comfortable for you, but it is a necessary step.

*Won't I lose clients?* Oh yes, you will. In fact, you may lose all your old clients. But you will not get high-paying clients if you don't lose at least some of your old clients. This is why you have to be strategic about how and when you increase your price.

More importantly, don't just ditch old clients who can't pay your new price. Create an option of some sort for them and be sure you leave on good terms. This doesn't mean some won't be irrationally angry with you. If you have a running contract, honor the terms of the contract till the end of it. Just don't sign a new one with the old rates.

If you are scared about increasing your price just like that, there is a way to feel better about it. Enroll in expensive training in your niche and pay for it in full with your savings. After such an experience, you won't have any qualms about increasing your price.

Make a decision to take at least one of these steps to increase how much you are worth by 10.

# CHAPTER 14: 13 SMALL CHANGES THAT MAKE A BIG DIFFERENCE

If there is one thing I hope you have learned so far, it is this: Getting rich is all about becoming like the rich.

That pretty much summarizes it. And you can start making changes to your life that can transport you into that state of wealth that you hope to be. Nobody knows what you want better than you. And there is a limit to how far you can go by copying the methods of other people.

Here are 13 changes you can make to your personal outlook that make a lot of difference. These changes can look small and insignificant but they are actually very powerful. Don't make excuses. Don't procrastinate. Just get going and make the changes that pertain to you.

## 1. Take a Professional Picture

You need to look like where you are going. Look less like where you are coming from and more like where you are going. Almost all business people judge anyone they are meeting for the first time based on their appearance. Since people cannot see you physically initially, they will draw conclusions from your photo. And you need to give a good impression of yourself.

Your picture should show your face as clearly as possible. Be careful with the editing: you don't want to create a photo that's different from what you look like in the real world. The point is not about showing the world how pretty or handsome you are. It is about having a face with which they can associate their thoughts about you.

How you dress is also important. Dress code can vary depending on your line of work. However, your attire must be neat and consistent with the new image of yourself you are trying to create.

Your facial expression also matters. The most common for professional photos is a smile. And that can be either a small smile or a big smile. But other expressions may be preferable, depending on your line of work. For example, a big smile is not the way to go if you're a lawyer. People want a badass lawyer, not a friendly one.

## 2. Buy a Publicly Visible Wealth Trigger

Wealth triggers are objects or items of luxury (subject to your level of affordability) that bring your future life to the present. This could be a wardrobe accessory like a pair of shoes, a necklace, or a watch. It could be something that you can place on a wall in your house and office. It could be artwork you place on your desk. It just has to be something that reminds you of your new self-image.

Have you seen people who are more dignified and confident in their behavior when they are impeccably dressed? It is a way of influencing your personality, of hacking your behavior. Every time you are tempted to think low, it forces you to think otherwise.

You will surely outgrow something like this, but it is instrumental in the early stages.

### 3. Express Gratitude Towards Someone Whose Content Has Provided You Value

Email works for this in most cases. Write an email to someone whose content has helped you achieve something. Or maybe there is a book you once read that helped you. Find the author and write an email.

Don't start with this book. Think further back and think of someone whose content has helped you. If you can think of 20 authors, get their email addresses and write to them. Give honest and sincere appreciation. Good things will come from it.

Some may not reply. In fact, many may not reply. But the process of writing will unveil some important things to you. Also, if you get a response, it will change your paradigm somehow.

### 4. Make Daily Affirmations

Daily affirmations are positive words of confidence you say

about yourself to yourself. The purpose is to condition your subconscious mind for the life you want.

For example, I say to myself every morning:

"I am super-rich!"

And when I say it, I say it with an attitude and involve my emotions. There is a list of statements I make every morning. And I will keep saying them every morning. I tell my mind where I want to go.

You need daily affirmations to keep your mind focused on your goals and desires. It may seem like a small thing, but those few minutes of spoken words every day make a lot of difference.

## 5. Take a Senior Colleague to Lunch

This is a good stunt. Position yourself for better and greater responsibilities by solidifying relationships with those who are where you want to be. Take senior colleagues to lunch (and of course you pay).

Another smart thing to do is to ask important work questions over lunch. Do this in a friendly and relaxed way; it must look more like a chat than an interview. You would be surprised how much this singular act can bring you.

## 6. Introduce Yourself to Your Boss's Boss

There is always an occasion that is right for this. This is for people whose progress depends on promotion at the workplace. How can the person at the top promote you if they don't know you?

First, you have to do something that makes you stand out from everybody else. Then you should find a way to let those at the top know it.

Don't just walk up and introduce yourself by mentioning your name. Mention a result that you are directly responsible for. Sometimes it is good to mention that before you say your name.

## 7. Dress for Success

A young intern started working at an office in a big city. But she had a problem. The main staff members kept sending her out on food errands. She hated it. So a consultant gave her a piece of advice. He told her to start wearing heels to work.

She took his advice, and the errands stopped. The intern was so surprised. Nobody said anything about her change in shoes, but the errands just stopped. One day, she got tired of the heels and wore flat shoes to work again. The errands resumed that day.

Dress for success. You don't have to be extravagant, you just have to look the way you want people to see you.

## 8. Start Your Day Earlier Than Your Colleagues

This is a bit straightforward. There is something about punctuality that fosters leadership. When you start work earlier than your colleagues you are more likely to be considered for a leadership position before any of them.

If they start work by 8:30 am, you start by 8:00 am. Always strive to be ahead. Sometimes this could work in the inverse. An example is showing up to work 2 hours late but with 4 hours of work done already.

## 9. Change Long Emails to Calls

Short emails are good. Chats and messaging are also good. But when it comes to long discussions, there is nothing like a phone call. Don't do long emails, just schedule a call.

There are lots of online platforms that make calls over the internet possible such as Skype and Zoom. Calls also make the person you are communicating with value your discussion even more.

## 10. Set Aside Time Every Day to Think

People live on autopilot. They just keep living their lives without stopping to think about what they really want from life. Some think once they have determined what they want, they don't need to rethink it. No.

The journey of self-discovery has no end. Give yourself time each day to detach from your current situation and think. Thinking doesn't mean reflecting on your life and your past decisions. Thinking means projecting your future and checking if you are still on the right track to attain what you want.

Thinking is important because shortcuts open up in life from time to time. And if you are too busy living to pay attention, you will miss those opportunities.

And there are also traps that appear as opportunities. If you don't think carefully about them and just keep making default decisions, you will fall into those traps.

## 11. Talk About Your Successes

People who talk about failure attract more of it. Those who talk about success attract more of it. In the desire to be funny, people often talk themselves down. They magnify their failures and make themselves look like fools.

Don't do that. Talk about your successes. It may not be funny, but it will cause people to have confidence in your ability to deliver. There is also a graceful way to talk about your failures. Talk about the failure, and then follow it up with a success story.

## 12. Reject More Offers

Don't let people reject you all the time. Also, learn to politely reject good offers. When you start looking successful, offers will start rolling in. You should reject most of them. It increases your confidence. Most of the offers won't be what you want to do anyway.

Rejecting an offer doesn't mean you should make an enemy of

the one doing the offering. Don't insult people. Don't make any-one feel like a fool for reaching out to you. Decline politely.

## 13. Practice in Front of the Mirror

When you are involved in something that has to do with re-questing or receiving money, you need to practice mentioning the price. When you mention the price, you must not show any sign of excitement or disbelief. You should be able to name your price with a straight face.

You might think this is easy. But go try it in front of a mirror and you will see how your body language can betray you. This is im-portant especially if you are talking about big figures.

Whenever you have a meeting, whether real or virtual, practice in front of the mirror beforehand. Practice until your body lan-guage doesn't give you away. Don't assume that your body lan-guage will just be better without any practice. It won't.

Implement as many of these things as you can. They will make a huge difference and make you more successful.

# CHAPTER 15: STARTING
# WITH NO MENTORS

The alternative to mentorship that you can use to rise in status and get rich is a good reputation. A good reputation is a capital resource. It is more powerful than money because it can create money. Focus first on building your reputation, and your journey to getting rich (without a mentor) will be so much easier.

People often think of a reputation as something you build after you have made money. This is the idea the media promotes, and a lot of people tend to view it as common sense.

But the problem with this manner of thinking is that it sends people on an unnecessarily difficult journey early in life. For example, it makes them believe they have to make a lot of money before they can help others. And this is not true.

It is in trying to meet the needs of other people that we discover the mission that gives us the reputation we desire. And that good reputation can then be used as the starting point on our journey to riches.

This is the way life works. But many just ignore it. They start their lives focused on the wrong things and life becomes a struggle.

A good reputation makes life easy. But it doesn't come naturally. What does come naturally is a reputation for being a nice or kind person. And that is not so useful in the business world. In fact, it can be a disadvantage because people will try to take advantage of you.

You have to intentionally create a good reputation by doing things that give you a good name in society. It is easier to translate that into wealth than to start trying to get rich from scratch.

## Don't Start Your Career Chasing Money

When most people begin life after school, their first priority is often to earn money. This could be because they need to pay off their accumulated debt. It could be because of the lifestyle that they have to sustain by themselves. It could be to keep up with the Joneses.

To make matters worse, they look for jobs that position them to earn. The moment you start working for money, you have positioned yourself as a servant of money.

People change jobs just because they get another offer with higher pay. They are lured into bigger and bigger responsibilities by the promise of more money. The problem with having money like that is that you have traded away your time and energy for it.

People don't get rich by working harder. They may end up with a fair amount of money, but they will have traded the time and energy they would have used to enjoy it.

This is not to say that any attempt to get a job after school is wrong. Instead, it is to show you that money is not the right reason to accept a job offer. You can consider the money, but it should not be among your top priorities.

## Prioritize Reputation Over Money

It is not about who is offering you more money. Instead, it is about where you can build your reputation. Money is important, but reputation is more important.

The question you should ask yourself is this:

Can I stock up public victories, success stories, and testimonials for myself in this place?

Before you venture into any business, you must consider this for yourself. The first business you do likely will not be the one that will make you huge money. But you will need the success stories from that first business to leverage when a huge opportunity shows up.

You can prioritize money over reputation if your mentor (who has achieved what you hope to achieve) is telling you to follow that path. But if you have no mentor to guide you, it is better to prioritize your reputation first.

Prioritizing your reputation means to focus on doing something that will make you recognizable (in a good way) in your society.

## Better Than Mentorship?

Mentorship has no substitutes. Even if you don't have a mentor today, you may have one in the future. So, this is not against the idea of having mentors. However, there are alternatives to mentorship that will bring you to the same destination.

Mentorship just makes the journey easier. It is very easy if you follow in the steps of someone who has done something you want to do.

The mistake people make is when it comes to choosing their mentors. They make mentors of people who have not achieved what they want. Those people might be successful in something else, but a person is only qualified to be your mentor if they have achieved what you hope to achieve.

You can have teachers. You can have a few people you learn from on a regular basis. You can even have a person you write personal accountability reports to every week. But all of that is different from mentorship.

A mentor is someone who shows you what steps to take. A mentor is someone whose moves you copy. That is why success is easy with a mentor. But if you can't find one, that doesn't mean you can't achieve what you want.

Building a reputation is better than mentorship because it makes you a leader very quickly when you get to the top.

## Reputation Will Make You More
## Money Over the Long Run

When you begin your business career by choosing reputation over money, it might seem like you are throwing money away. But if you stick to this, it will make you a lot more money in the long run.

Money is good and it can open almost any door in the world. But there are some doors that you will be entirely oblivious of if you don't have social capital.

If you are standing before a door and you want it opened, money can open it if used in the right way. But a good reputation will show and unlock doors that you would have otherwise mistaken for walls.

If you are not shown certain opportunities, you will never know they exist. And you won't get any reasonable response if you try to inquire about them. The only way in is when your reputation is large enough to make those in the know invite you in.

In the end, focusing on a good reputation will make you more money than if you had just gone blindly chasing after money. It will get you to the goal even though it is a more adventurous path than mentorship.

## Money Chases Reputation

Investors are always looking for people who have had 2 or 3 successful startups and want to start another one. The investors know that such people are the least risky individuals to bet on.

This is why some smart entrepreneurs bootstrap their first startup, scale it, and then sell it. After that first success, they go around tooting their horns for a bit. Then they raise money for another startup, build, and sell again. The media celebrates their achievements as startup entrepreneurs. Then they get to the point where they can raise billions.

Money follows reputation. If you have a reputation, you won't have to beg for the money to get it. In fact, people will chase you down with money.

If you chase a good reputation, the money will chase you. Work to become well known.

## Do More Things That Give You a Name

If you have no mentors, then you should concentrate on doing things that set you on a higher plane in society. You may have to start with very small things. But soon enough they will become big things.

The "building a reputation" here is slightly different from how it is generally understood. It doesn't entail things like running a charitable foundation or leading the support for a legislative bill. Let me elaborate:

Say you want to hire someone for a senior post in your tech company and you have 2 candidates who both fit and are pretty much similar in every respect. But the only difference is that one previously worked for Google while the other doesn't have any big tech company experience. That immediately makes your choice obvious, doesn't it?

Reputation is about what makes you recognizable as someone who can deliver results. And it can be achieved in many ways: work experience (like the Google example), writing, speaking, organizing, and generally being a part of successful ventures.

Before you pick up any responsibility at the early stage of your business career, ask yourself:

Will this increase my reputation?

Another way of looking at reputation is the phrase "street credibility." If you have no mentors, you start out by stacking up your street credibility. Once you have a bunch of it, doors of opportunities will naturally begin to open.

This is how to become rich if you have no mentor. You can't go wrong by building a good business reputation. It can be a long journey, but you will eventually get to the same destination.

If you have a mentor, just do what your mentor says.

# PART IV: DEALING WITH DEBTS

They offered to take my gut feeling, creativity, and

freedom. In exchange, they would give me maximum

security, fear, and a fancy paper. Plus, I would owe

them $150K. I stormed out of the meeting.

# CHAPTER 16: GETTING RID OF
# THE DEBTS THAT WORRY YOU

I f a particular debt is making you worry, then you should pay it off as soon as you can.

No debt is worth the trade-off for your peace of mind. You must put your mental wellbeing before your financial life. In fact, your mental wellbeing has a direct influence on your financial life. You can't make good decisions in your finances if your mind is not at peace.

Forget about trying to play smart and take advantage of the market. If you have the mental headspace for it, and you have the financial education to pull it off, then do it.

But if you don't, it is not wise to force yourself into the zone. Play at your own pace.

There are two kinds of debt—good debt and bad debt. Bad debt means that the debt does not pay for itself. Only a bad debt should make you worry.

What the banking system calls bad debt is debt that the debtor cannot repay. Or debt that the debtor has already defaulted in paying. But for you to have a good personal finance experience, I define bad debt as debt that you have to repay from somewhere else.

Let's say you take on debt to buy a car. My question then is: will that car repay the debt? Or will you have to repay the debt from something else?

Let's say you bought the car to be more productive at work. If that resulting productivity brings you an additional income large enough to cover the monthly repayments (and car maintenance), then that is good debt (in a personal finance sense). But if not, it is bad debt.

You should only go into debt for things that promise to increase your income. If there is no clear pathway for something to increase your income, you should not get into debt for it.

Good debts don't make people worry. Only bad debt does this. And there is a pathway that can lead to the eradication of all such debts. But first, you need to understand something.

## Your Debts Are Not as Big as You Think They Are

The first problem is your perception. How big do you think your debt is? This is not really about the amount. This is about what that amount is to you.

Someone can have a debt of $500K in San Francisco (USA) and believe it is no big deal. Meanwhile, another person can have a $50K debt in Accra (Ghana), and it is a major source of worry.

How big is your debt relative to where you currently are in life?

If you worry a lot about your debt, that means the size is overwhelming.

The reason the debt looks overwhelming is because of where you are standing and looking at it from. If you change your position, suddenly the size of the debt changes.

The amount doesn't go down, but it looks much smaller than it initially appeared.

For example, if you are a small business owner, a $50K debt looks overwhelming. It looks that way because you have chosen to stick with the identity of "small business owner."

The moment you shift your perception and start seeing yourself as a medium-size business owner, the way you see the debt changes. And then you realize that the debt isn't really that huge.

## You Are Thinking Too Small

A $5K debt will look like a huge sum if all you earn in a month is less than $500. Just like the $50K debt looks huge to the small business owner. But the moment you start making plans to hit $3M in revenue next year, that $50K debt becomes small.

Your debt problem is not the size of the debt. Your debt problem is due to the fact that you are thinking too small.

Think bigger than your debts. Multiple times bigger.

In fact, this small thinking is what brought you to the place where you have these worrisome debts. If you had applied a macro-thinking approach, the debts wouldn't be this disturbing.

Small thinking is not just in terms of money size, it is also in terms of timelines. People get into debt looking only at the short-term. They do not visualize for the next 10 years, 20 years, 50 years.

Your decisions today are shaping the coming decades of your life. If you are not thinking about those decades now, you will not like what they have to offer when they finally arrive.

Your small thinking is also what is making you worry. If you have a concept of the big picture and you fix your gaze on it, the worry evaporates.

Keep your eye on the big picture.

## Dream 10x

This is how I recommend you start dealing with debts that make you worry.

1. Sum up all those debts
2. Multiply by 10
3. Aim for that as your income goal

Dream 10x your current state. And don't just wish for it—get serious with it. Start chasing that dream.

You may think achieving it is impossible, but just believe you can and get started.

Imagine the lifestyle that brings such income and internalize it for yourself. Embrace the work ethic that produces such income. Go and familiarize yourself with environments where people who make such income abound.

Dream way bigger than your debts and take action on your dream every day.

## You Don't Have a Debt Problem, You Have an Income Problem

Debt is not your problem. There is no one in the world who has a debt problem. The only problem is income. If your income can cover your debt comfortably, then you have no problem.

The problem with debt is when your income is not enough to repay it. So, the debt is not the issue. That is why there is good debt and bad debt.

Focus on how you can expand your income. Focus on how to get your revenue higher. Only cash inflow can solve your debt problem. Worrying about the debt won't.

Beware of thinking too much about the debt. It will only drag you further down. Instead, write down all of the ways cash flows to you. Then think of how you can increase the number of ways.

## Set an Income Goal

There is more that goes into setting an income goal than just a number. It's good to have a number to aim for, but you need all the other strategies.

Only remember that what you know in your head will not change your situation; it is what you practice that will change your situation. More about this in the next chapter.


## Make Better Decisions Next Time

The debt in which you currently are is a result of your past decisions. If you don't change your way of thinking, you will find yourself with the same problem again.

This is why you need to upgrade your way of thinking. Do this by upgrading what you listen to and what you read.

The first step in achieving this is to eliminate the things you read and listen to that drag you under. Instead, read and listen to things that set you up high where you want to go.

If you don't upgrade your thinking, you will continually create this kind of debt problem for yourself.

Also, you need to re-educate yourself about money and personal finance. Learn how to use good debt as leverage. Debt is not bad or evil. It only depends on the financial education of the person using it.

The only way to make better decisions next time is to upgrade your way of thinking.

## Having a Way to Pay Is Peace of Mind

What evaporates the worries and gives you peace of mind is not really the payment of the debts. Instead, it is when you have an assured way to pay.

When the money is flowing in large quantities, your worry disappears. If you have money flowing in but it's barely enough to pay the monthly debt repayment, there is still a reason to worry.

Worry disappears when you have income from multiple sources producing at least 5x your total debt. Just the thought of this income, or even a strategy to implement it, will give you peace of mind.

Stop worrying about your debts; instead, think of how to increase your income, and then take action on those thoughts.

# CHAPTER 17: HOW TO SET AN INCOME GOAL AND SURPASS IT

The hardest part of achieving an income goal is first believing you can get there. Most people shoot themselves in the foot when they get close.

Your income is not just an amount of money. It is also your mental comfort zone when it comes to money. Everyone who works and gets paid has an amount beyond which they would be uncomfortable receiving.

We have been trained through school to go step by step to achieve our goals. This structure is fixed in our minds even after school. We only aspire as high as the next position on the job ladder we are on. We never think of scaling beyond to earn more money than our boss's boss.

That thought is just too far away. Some would even think it is inappropriate. And just by that type of thinking, people remain fixed on a certain income level.

◆ ◆ ◆

What about those who are paid on commission? In most organizations like that, the sales manager can easily tell what a particular salesperson will make in a month. They just look at how much they have made in the past months.

In most cases, the income stays consistent. Even if the salesperson reaches their usual number in the first week, the next 3 weeks will see no increase. This is because their income level is a fence in their minds. They seem unable to go beyond it easily.

What is your income fence? Many people say they want more money. But they are not ready to associate with the new income they want. In fact, the amount they want scares them. Deep down they know that such an amount is not for them.

You can earn as much money you want. But you have to believe you can get there first. You would be surprised how afraid people are of earning more money. People are afraid to earn more money than their parents.

People are scared of success more than failure. This is because they know that along with success comes the spotlight and responsibilities. Every new income level gives you a different responsibility. If you are scared of the responsibility you know is coming, you will unconsciously find ways to sabotage yourself from getting that new income.

The new income level that you want is not just about the money. It is also about lifestyle and responsibilities. Are you willing to change?

For most people, they know what to do to get the income they desire. But they are scared of having the position that brings the income. If you desire the income and you don't want the responsibility, you won't get the income.

This mindset shift is the first stage.

Your current income is based on your current self-image. Unless you change your self-image, none of the changes you make will lead to sustainable additional income.

Your self-image is the first thing you alter. You have to see yourself as someone in the higher tiers of earning. Otherwise, you will never get there. If you get there by accident, you won't stay there.

## Something About You Has to Change

Increasing your income is not primarily about the money you want. It is more about the person you currently are. If you want to earn more than you currently do, something about you has to change.

On a personal basis, you have to change your self-image. This is how you see yourself. For example, if you are earning $3K a month and you want to start earning $10K, you have to start seeing yourself as someone earning $10K.

You have to literally start treating yourself as someone earning $10K. And it is going to be hard at first. This is because your mind will keep trying to drag you backward.

You have to internalize that frame of mind to the point that the people around you notice something different about you. The easiest way to earn $10K a month from $3K is to become the person who earns such an amount.

Ask yourself, how would I live if I earned $10K a month? You may not be able to afford all of what that entails, but you can re-structure your mindset to fit into that new image.

Your mindset does not know what is real and what is not real. If you mentally take yourself to the mindset of the rich and stay there long enough, the opportunities will come to you.

Another thing that needs to change is your positioning. How have you positioned yourself in the workplace? You should put yourself in a position where people assume you are the boss.

Take your appearance seriously. Walk 25% faster. Make decisions. Take initiative. Become the problem solver, not the person who sends problems to other people.

Your work ethics must also change if you have a bad work ethic. If you are always making excuses, you should stop. Don't make excuses, just figure out how to get the job done.

In some cases, you might need to change your workplace. You must be open to that also. If you want a better income you must make sure you are in the right company or organization that can lead you to it.

At least one thing will have to change. You must be ready for that change and make it happen.

## Add to What You Know

You may be wondering why we have not talked about the figures. The reason is that a figure is useless without everything we have just mentioned. That is why people set income goals and do not achieve them.

Another important point in changing your income is adding to what you know. Your income is where it is today because of what you know. Knowledge is increasing every day. Businesses need people with that knowledge to give them that edge.

If you have not unlearned and relearned anything in the last 18 months, you are not taking your professional life seriously. If you desire a new income, you should learn what people who are already earning it know.

Nobody will pay you 10 times what you earn now for the present level of knowledge you function with. You need to add to your knowledge base.

This is not about adding anything you feel like. Do research on people earning what you want. Find out what they know that you don't. Or perhaps what they are known for. Then, become one of them.

A decision to increase your knowledge is a decision to increase your income.

## Have a Definite Eventual Target

What income will be enough for you? Sadly, many people do not have a definite answer for this. They just keep going for more and more until they run out of steam.

What is your dream income? This is not about mentioning a figure that sounds big. This is about examining the kind of life you want.

Think about the life you want. How much do you need to be making in a month to afford it?

You need to have a target in sight. There will be steps and levels on the way there. But you need to have an end target. If not, you will not enjoy your progress in life.

Determine the life you want and know the income goal you need to set. Don't just pick a random number from your head. It may be a mild estimation, but you need to make an informed decision.

It is important to know what you want.

## Celebrate Milestones and Every Major Progress

If your goal is $10K and you are at $3K, you must learn to celebrate every significant increase. For example, when you get to $5K, you must celebrate your progress.

Celebrating your progress means doing something you have

predetermined to do with the extra money. It could be buying something, taking your family on a trip, or anything.

What you do has to be a reward to yourself for the progress you have made.

This stage is very important. Chasing an income goal without connecting something significant to the income will result in emptiness. Your income goal must be tied to something that gives you fulfillment and happiness.

The point here is that you don't have to wait to get to your final goal before you allow yourself to celebrate. Every major stride you make ought to be celebrated.

This encourages you to keep going forward.

## Create New Work Principles and Routines for Yourself

You cannot sustain your old routine and achieve a new income goal. Your routine has to change. You also need to create new principles for how you work.

Your goal will require a new structure for how you spend your day. You might need to delegate less important tasks. You might need to hire an assistant. You might need to work longer hours. Or even add an afternoon nap to your schedule so you stay fresh.

You will definitely need new routines. You can't remain who you were and expect to be rewarded with more. Most people who get promoted in an organization start doing the work their new level of promotion requires before they are promoted. Think about that.

## Have Your Eventual Goal in a Sharable Form

You should know the exact figure of your income goal. It is not necessary for you to share it. But you need to share something.

You need to present your income goal in a form that you can share with everybody. It is not so nice to mention the exact figures. This is because the figures can mean different things to different people. You want to avoid people projecting their ideals of that amount of money on you.

The way I share my income goals is in the form of where I want to live. I paint a clear picture of where I want to live for other people. I don't mention the actual figures.

In reality, the figures can change. But the dream remains constant until you achieve it. Tell people something about the life you want that gives them an idea of the income you are aiming for.

Interestingly, when you tell people about the life you are aiming for, they don't ask you about the numbers. They just get it.

To sum up, how do you set an income goal and achieve it?

- Know the dream life you want
- Set an income goal based on your dream life
- Upgrade your lifestyle (positioning, work ethic, routine, knowledge, etc.) and your self-image to fit your goal
- Have your goal in a sharable form

- Celebrate major progress
- Keep going!

As a final tip, the opportunity to get a major boost in income is sometimes disguised as work. The kind of work nobody wants to do. Here is a super-secret:

Work hard when everybody else is taking it easy.

And your hard work will show in the results you get. Don't boast of how hard you work. Boast of the results you get.

Surpassing your income goal is not something you consciously do. It is something that just happens if you are really committed to reaching your goals.

# CHAPTER 18: INTRODUCTION TO GOOD DEBT

They don't want you to be rich. They are trying to protect you from success as well as failure.

It is almost like they all gathered and held a meeting about it. "They" in this case include your parents, relatives, schoolteachers, college professors, politicians, and more. These are people who consider your safety more important than your dream. If any of those people taught you differently about debt, they deserve a medal of honor.

There is only one place to learn about success. And it is from someone who has been successful. The one who hasn't taken big risks, the one who hasn't made tough business choices, will only teach you to do the same.

Oftentimes, people advise others to become like them. This can be good or bad depending on who is giving the advice. Only people who have tasted real success can tell you what the road is actually like.

Most of us are misled about money very early in life. And we continue on that path because we know no other path. Conventional wisdom about money will make anyone poor.

When people are on the verge of waking up to the reality of their wrong paths, politicians arise to mislead them with the fake and impossible promises of making debts disappear, making everything free, and zero consequence for bad money choices. Honest, successful people don't like such campaign promises because success has taught them differently.

Money is an important subject. You can't truly understand money until you understand debt. Money is not cash.

Less than 5% of the entire money in the world is in cash

They say money makes the world go round. But, in reality, debt makes the world go round. The US is the biggest debtor in the world. But it is also the biggest creditor in the world. *Why don't they just focus on paying their debts?* The real question is: do they have to?

In 2008 when the US economy crashed (which triggered a global recession), money was injected into the system by the Federal Reserve. Do the Federal Reserve have money stashed away somewhere? No! They control monetary policy. In other words, if they say $200B exists, it comes into existence.

Here is my point. They justified the money into the system by buying up debts. Meaning that money has become a derivative of debt. They took debt and pumped out money.

This is just to show you how powerful debt is. It is even more powerful than money because of today's financial system. But there is good news.

You can make it work for you. Using your hard work to earn money is an industrial-age mentality. Instead, you can use debt to build a fortune for yourself.

I know it sounds scary to some. I am also in the process of re-adjusting my thinking to become more and more comfortable with the idea. Debt can be a good thing if you know how to use it to your advantage.

## There Is Such a Thing as Good Debt

There is a difference between good debt and bad debt. All most people have experience with is bad debt. They don't know that debt can be good.

My definition of bad debt is a little different from how banks define it.

Bad debt is a debt that you have to pay back from somewhere else.

Let's say you take out a loan to buy a car. The value of the car drops from the moment you drive it out of the dealer's shop. You spend money on maintenance, fuel, and accessories. The car doesn't bring money into your account. The car only takes money out. And you have to pay back the car loan from the money you get from your job or business.

Why is this bad? If you suddenly lose your job or your business goes south, you won't be able to pay back the loan anymore.

Then, the debt becomes really bad. You cannot sell the car and make gains because the value of the car will have dropped.

Some might argue that the car will increase productivity, which will eventually lead to more money. That can be true. But not for everyone. The status of the debt doesn't change. It is still a debt that cannot pay itself.

Good debt is different. What makes debt good is not what it is used for. Rather, it is its capacity to be paid back with gains from what it is used for.

Good debt is a debt that pays for itself and leaves you with gains.

It is not about what you buy. Let's take the example of the car loan again. But this time, you lease the car out to a driver for one of these ride-sharing platforms (like Uber). Now your monthly return can pay for the monthly loan payments and leave some extra money in your hands. That is good debt.

The car loan example can be a basic one, but it is just to let you know that anything can be turned into an income-producing property. This method is most common with real estate.

Smart real estate investors take a loan to buy property, revamp the property, and put it on the rental market. And (if everything goes well) the rent from the property pays for the monthly loan payments with some leftovers for the investor to enjoy.

If the investor's monthly loan payment is $2,800 and the return from the rental property (minus maintenance) is $3,000 per month, that is an extra $200 for the investor to play with.

Now imagine if the monthly payment is $250K and the returns (minus maintenance) is $3M: that is some $2.75M to play with. Why shouldn't the investor do it again? That is some very good debt.

By the way, it takes skill and knowledge to be able to make a real estate investment profitable like this. Make sure you know the market backward and forward before you attempt such an investment.

## Getting a Loan is Easy When You Are Rich

There are two types of loans. Of course, there are many types under many classifications, but for our purposes there are two kinds that are of interest.

They are: secured loans and unsecured loans. You are probably already familiar with secured loans. Those were the ones I knew too. I was surprised to discover that unsecured loans exist. Some countries do not offer unsecured loans but I think all of the developed countries do.

You can read further and educate yourself about unsecured loans. But the major difference that stood out to me is that you don't need collateral for unsecured loans. However, there is a catch: not everybody can access unsecured loans. Or I should say that unsecured loans are not accessed the same way that secured loans are.

If you are rich, doors fly open for you. Getting a loan is easy when you are rich.

Banks love to give money to people who don't need it. Of course, the day you are in dire need of money, they will run from you. But there is a trick to making this work for you.

If you look and act like you don't need the money (and you make them chase you), you will get all the money you want. And if you maintain your reputation as someone that always delivers and makes repayments on time, the bankers will be your buddies.

Getting a loan is easy if you are rich. Or I should rephrase that:

Getting a loan is easy if you seem like a rich person to the bankers.

## Banks Want You to Borrow Money

In most developed countries, the interest rate for money kept in savings accounts is very low. In some countries, it is even negative. This means the saver is thrown under the bus, while the borrower is rewarded.

Working hard to earn money seems to be an expensive and in-efficient way to get money. Why labor with your hands, time, and sweat for money when you can just chat with some bankers and they can give you your annual salary in one afternoon to invest in a business?

I don't mean to demean hard work in any way. But you have to think about the spectrum you are coming from. Let's say you are working hard so that you can have enough money to invest so that you can gain passive income and be able to quit your job.

Why not skip that whole "job" step? Here is what I mean.

Get the money, work hard on your investments, and enjoy your life doing what you want! I believe work should be fulfilling. If you hate your job, why stay there and endure it? The reason most people endure their horrible job is that they fear the unknown.

But what if the unknown becomes known? This is where self-education comes in. Stay with your job if you find fulfillment in it. But if it is just about getting money for investments, banks will give you money.

In fact, they are more willing to give than you are to get it. The only reason they would turn you down is that they doubt your capability for paying them back because you don't seem rich enough to them. The same bankers that reject loan applications from a certain group of people meet with top business people to persuade them to come to take a loan in their bank.

You just need to be associated with the right kind of crowd.

## The Rich Use Debts to Buy Assets

My definition of an asset is consistent with Robert Kiyosaki's definition. Kiyosaki says an asset is that which puts money into your pocket. Any other benefit doesn't count. For example, if the house you live in doesn't bring you any revenue, it is not an asset.

The main thing that keeps people poor is that they spend money on things that take money out of their pockets. They spend money on things that put them in a position of paying rather than a position of receiving.

I have noticed that super-rich people have simple explanations. But the poor and middle class have complex explanations. Oftentimes, the purpose of complex explanations is to make people confused. When people are confused, they can't make decisions. If they don't make decisions for themselves, then they will follow through with the default choices of the crowd.

In the modern world, the difference between the rich and everybody else is this:

The rich know how to spend money, the average are taught to save money, and the poor don't know how to make money.

Both making money and saving money are good if you know the smart way to do it. But what makes a person get rich and stay rich is how they spend money.

The rich buy assets. Other people buy liabilities when they have money, hence digging themselves deeper into a hole. The rich buy things that put them on the receiving end of the financial system.

This doesn't mean you should check every purchase to make sure it lines up with this. Instead, it means that before you make any major purchase that puts you at the paying end, you should instead consider making a purchase that puts you on the receiving end.

In most cases, it is not about what you buy. Instead, it is about what you do with what you buy. Never forget that it takes skill to do this right. This is why educating yourself matters a lot.

## A $400K Funny Story

I heard this funny story about Donald Trump from way back when he was just a businessman.

I heard the story from another businessman who was chatting with a group of bankers when they told him about their ordeal with Trump.

According to the bankers, Trump had gone to their bank for a loan. They went through all the details and were going to approve it. Then Trump added an extra $400K for personal expenses.

The interesting thing to the bankers was that Trump said, "$400K for personal expenses," with a straight face. $400K was probably more than the annual salary of those bankers at that time. They were stunned that someone could ask for such a sum without his expression giving away the fact that he was trying to pull one over them. He was stern and serious.

The funny thing was that he got it. The bankers sheepishly admitted that they gave him the money.

Sometimes getting the money you want is all about how you look.

## Play the Game Before You Buy Your Dreams

People get into debt for ridiculous things. The most ridiculous, in my opinion, at this time is student loans. It is a dangerous trap.

Why are student loans a bad debt? Let us assume that the economy will always be good and you get a good job that only gets better. Let us also assume that you studied a great course in school that is in demand in the outside world. In the end, it doesn't put money in your pocket!

In the end, you get to trade your time and skills for money. If your education is really an asset worth taking out a loan for, why do you have to pay your time and exertion to turn it into money?

It is like you are paying the system to take time away from you, in hopes that you will receive more money for it later. That is not smart (in my opinion). Also, there is too much uncertainty in the world to take up debt based on the fact that it might enable you to find a high-paying job (and be in it long enough to fully pay back your loans).

Rushing out of debt isn't very smart either. Many people are rushing to get out of debt only to get into another bad debt. Change your thinking.

It is not about how to get out of debts; instead, it is about how can I have more good debts than bad debts?

The mindset of paying your debts will only bring you to zero.

Your fight will be to go from negative funds to zero. But having good debts is about fighting to get into the positive and stay there.

Just because you are reducing your debts doesn't mean you are making progress financially. Are you enjoying your life? Is your income becoming less tied to how much work you need to do physically?

Think of the financial world as a game. It is about making more money come to you than is being taken from you. Everybody has things they'd love to buy for themselves. But play the game first and get ahead, then you can buy anything you want.

# CHAPTER 19: 7 REASONS TO
# USE DEBT LIKE THE RICH

B anks and central banks have created a debt system for the rich to grow their wealth astronomically without involving their personal wealth. The system makes it possible to take advantage of the uncertain value of money, government policy, and even taxes to create new wealth.

In some cases, the assets of the rich are used as collateral against those loans. But unsecured loans require no collateral and can generate an infinite return based on the vision of the business or investment.

Suppose you have $4M in assets and you get $6M from a bank in a loan for a business deal. If the deal works out and you make a profit of $2M, your new capital base will basically be $12M.

This is why the rich keep using debt for their business. The growth of their wealth can be astronomical, and only limited by their minds, because banks are always willing to loan out money.

Banks always like to loan money to the rich. They know that with their wealth of experience, having created wealth several times before, it will be easy for them to do it again. They also see them as people who know how to get what they want. And finally, personal wealth gives the bankers security to hold on to in case the borrower fails to repay their loan.

The first two times dealing with banks are always the hardest. From then on it becomes easy because you get used to the hassle of dealing with them.

In further detail, here are 7 reasons the rich use debt for business:

## 1. Debt Is Money

In 1971, the then US President, Richard Nixon, took the dollar off the gold standard. This meant that the dollar was no longer a gold certificate. It also meant that the US could now print as many US dollars as needed to navigate any and every financial situation.

Whenever the economy is in trouble, the banks turn to the Federal Reserve for help. The Fed comes through for the banks. And then the banks come through for the rich. And the banks come through for the rich not because they are biased, but because only the rich have demonstrated creditworthiness on the level that impacts the banks.

Due to the fact that the dollar is not based on anything, it has ceased to be a store of value. It became useless to save it and hoard it because the value is no longer fixed. But it is smart to borrow it because as its value diminishes, what you ultimately pay will be less (relative to other assets and commodities).

Most other currencies of the world are pegged to the US dollar. And if the US dollar is now a debt certificate, virtually all currencies are the same.

Debt is now money. Government debt is called bonds. In a healthy economy, it makes more sense to own bonds than to own cash. If the government raises money by issuing bonds, why shouldn't the rich use debt?

## 2. Debt Is Cheap

Banks have a quota they must give out in loans every year. Loans are the primary way banks make money. The interest on those loans is their profit. So in order to make maximum gains each year, banks have to give a certain amount of loans out. Each bank has a target.

This puts them under more pressure to give than those who want to take the loans. Banks do know how to turn down unqualified applications, but they often run after qualified people. And those qualified people are the rich.

They offer these loans very cheaply to them. The bigger the loan, the cheaper the interest on it is. So, why use your own wealth on your latest business venture when you can get the money at a cheap rate from a bank?

It is cheaper to use debt than to use your own money.

### 3. Debt Is Less Risky

To someone who doesn't have the financial education, using debt to invest or for business is very risky. But to someone who has dedicated themselves to their financial education, the risk is much less.

When using your own personal wealth for any project, you are going to be overly careful and try to be as economical as possible. As a consequence, you might try to save money by neglecting some expenses that will come back to haunt you later. For example, you may try to go cheap on the insurance, and then the very event that you skimped on covering happens.

When you are spending the bank's money, you have no reason to hold back. Everything is already factored into the loan. Using debt for the business venture is way less risky.

Also, if the business fails, the debt is on the corporate entity and not on the individual. If the company is well structured, the individual is in less trouble than they would have been if the business was financed by their own personal fortune.

### 4. Debt Gives More Leverage

Leverage is a concept borrowed from engineering. In simplified terms, leverage makes it possible to move a huge load with much less effort. It usually involves a mechanical setup like a crowbar. A tiny effort can move anything if it gets a big enough leverage.

Debt is the leverage of the financial world. With your own personal wealth, you can double or triple what you have. But if you use debt, then insanely large multiples become possible. You can do 25x, 100x, 500x, and more.

This is what the entire stock derivatives market is based on. But it is risky, as failure can be devastating.

In other less risky investments, debt gives decent leverage. The best leverage is on a business where the financial outcome is based on skills and competence.

## 5. There Is an Abundance of Lenders

Using debt for business would be hard if loans were hard to get. But there is an abundance of lenders. Banks are everywhere. And as long as you look like someone rich and competent, they will give you money.

And if you don't take the money, others will. And the money might end up in the hands of the wrong people who will then squander it. So, if you are a good businessperson, you are doing society some good by taking the money banks offer you.

The rich use debt because it's easy money, and there are lots of places you can get it.

## 6. Using Debt Exercises Money Skills

Using your personal wealth requires no financial education. You just write a check and that is it. But if you are going to take on debt, you need to be at the top of your game.

Taking on debt requires being up to date with banking laws, government policies, taxes, and a lot of other things. In some cases, it requires partnering up with someone else to be able to draw out finances from the bank. All these make you sharp and on top of your game in business. And staying sharp is very important.

The decision not to use debt puts you out of the money game in this world. The big players use debt, and that is why they are on top of the game. Rich businesspeople stop using debt only when they are planning for retirement.

## 7. They Get to Keep Their Own Money

Imagine you keep your wealth in an asset yielding 10% per year. Why would you take it out so you can finance another venture that will yield almost the same rate?

The rich take on debt based on that asset. Then they are able to keep the asset, which still produces income and grows year after year. Then the second asset can grow without touching the first asset because of the use of debt.

The top reason rich businesspeople use debt to finance their next business venture is that they get to keep all their previous assets up and functioning. They can build a second and a third business without touching funds from their first business.

This is why the rich keep getting richer.

Money is not something you stockpile anymore. It has become something transactional. You use money up because there will always be an abundance of it.

The rich use debt because debt is money. You ought to grow to the point where you can do the same.

# CHAPTER 20: 7 LESSONS
## ABOUT POSITIONING

**M**oney loves the rich. But poor and middle-class people hate money. How? I'm glad you asked.

The conventional wisdom is that the rich like money. That they are greedy and obsessed with having more money. That may be true in some cases. But in most cases, it is money that looks out for the rich.

Meanwhile, poor and middle-class people are driven to action by their lack of money. They want to do things that will be rewarded in money. They often complain about their lack of money and hence express hate for money.

People who don't have enough money often think they are better people than those who do. They assume that their lack of massive wealth makes them more human and lets them enjoy life more. But it is just a lie they made up in their heads.

Money tests and proves character. You don't really know who a person is until the person has massive wealth. Wealth is like an amplifier. If you are a good person, wealth amplifies it. If you are a bad person, wealth amplifies it.

If you are a good person, why not desire to have it amplified?

Rich people grow richer because they keep playing the game of money. It is not really because they want more money. Instead, it is because the game is fun. For many of them, it is a game of real-life monopoly.

There are ways the rich position and condition themselves for more wealth and riches. It is how they attract more money. These ways and methods are things you probably see and haven't read much into. But they are very intentional moves.

Definitely, there are some exceptions. There are rich people who don't do any of the things listed here. But if you dig deeper into their lives, you will find out something they do that is based on one of the concepts listed.

Also, there are those who do a combination of these things. And the end result is even more opportunities and money. So, here you go:

## 1. They Surround Themselves With Wealth Triggers

A wealth trigger is something that constantly reminds you of your state of wealth. It is something that puts you in an unconscious mental state of abundance. It could be anything. But it is often a work of art, picture, relic, or design.

Some people even keep cash around as a wealth trigger. They surround themselves with things that inspire them to live their best. In some cases, it is something that has a rich history.

Super-rich fund managers are often fond of artwork. Some have art collections to the tune of hundreds of millions. Gazing at such expensive works of art gives the positive vibe of wealth.

The interior design of the offices and homes of the rich is often designed to trigger a mindset of prosperity and abundance. This keeps their minds in an unconscious state of abundance. And this attracts money.

Also, people who come to visit feel the "abundance energy" in the living space around them and desire to do business with them based on that. And in some cases, the visitors don't even consciously notice it.

## 2. They Dress Rich

Dressing rich is not the same as dressing expensively. You can dress expensively and look like a spoilt brat. Dressing rich is very different.

Dressing rich is all about looking admirable. It is about looking like you live in abundance. It is different from showing off. When you show off, you are trying to look superior to the other person.

It is better to dress to impress than to show off. And that means dress to give a powerful first impression. But this is also different from dressing rich. The concept of dressing rich is dressing to be in an abundance mood.

Many rich people think of their dress style as their own super-hero costume. So every day they dress with the intention of putting themselves in a power mood to make things happen. In their costume, they can walk up to anybody and react to anything.

The dress style of the rich is to persuade themselves of their state. They dress to give themselves the esteem and confidence to face the business world every day. Dressing rich is expensive, but it is not done to impress others; rather, it is to add to their own boldness to take every opportunity that comes their way.

The rich dress in such a way that if they meet another rich person they've always wanted to do business with, they can walk up to them without any hesitation.

### 3. They Give Away Money

Philanthropy is a very powerful thing. Yes, it is one of the ways the rich buy goodwill from society. But that is not all there is to it.

Life is actually measured by how much you give, not how much you make.

Billionaires are not stupid when they make huge donations or pledge their wealth to a charitable cause. One of the ways to show that you are not enslaved by money is to give it away.

So, how does that make a rich person richer? Good question. Not all wealth is financial. Giving money away is a way of buying happiness.

Happiness does not have a price tag, but money can buy it. And you don't have to be super-rich to do it. Have you ever given someone money or bought something for someone and their excitement at receiving your gift gave you goosebumps? It is an amazing feeling. The feeling that you are an answer to someone's prayer.

This act puts your mind in a state of bliss. One simple act like that can make you happy for a whole week. This is how money buys happiness.

When you are happy, you make better decisions. You see more opportunities. The world smiles at you.

## 4. They Integrate Their Tasks

Discipline is such a big word in personal development. But it is the most challenging for people. Discipline is hard. Motivation makes it seem like discipline is the answer. And motivation gets you going for the first few days. But then life blows distractions your way and you don't even notice when you go 2 weeks without thinking about your new resolution or decision.

Rich people are humans too. They want the end result of all that discipline and motivation. They love end results. But they hate the ugly work involved. There is always some ugly aspect of the work that isn't enjoyable at all. So, how do they get through that?

Discipline is good but it is not sustainable. There will be days where the discipline is broken. This is why rich people integrate their tasks into their lives. Here is how it works.

Integration is structuring your environment and time to force you to do certain tasks. A young millionaire forces himself to work out by having a gym in his house. At the time stipulated for workouts, he has a workout group that shows up to his house. By the time his gym buddies show up to his house for a workout session, he has to join them. They hold him accountable for his decision to have a workout session at the time set aside for it.

Integration means organizing your environment and schedule to make default decisions for you. With discipline, you have to decide or choose to do something every day. With integration, you make no decisions. You are forced to do it.

Integration is a combination of creating a system that cancels all barriers to doing the task and creating an effective system that keeps you accountable. It is how the rich get going when the going gets tough. Regular people often trust their discipline and it fails.

Integration makes the rich richer because it keeps them going when it gets difficult and depressing. In a lot of cases, success is a product of consistency.

## 5. They Change Failure Elements in Their Environment

I read about a billionaire who stopped wearing pink ties because he lost a court case the first day he officially wore one. What has the color of a tie got to do with a legal case? It may look weird to you, but it is the way the rich think.

Rich businesspeople cut their losses very quickly. And these losses are not limited to contracts and deals. It concerns every-thing in their environment. If something, no matter how good it is, seems like a bad omen, they remove it from their lives. This is why most ultra-rich people have some really weird preferences.

If they buy a car and take it out to seal a business deal for the first time and the deal goes sour, they might sell the car. Or vow never to take it out again.

The rich remove from their environment the things that re-mind them of their past failures.

So, it is not just about surrounding themselves with things that set their minds on good luck, favor, and abundance. It is also about removing anything that contradicts it. It doesn't matter how small.

## 6. They Make Sure Great Results Can Be Traced Back to Them

The rich are bold enough to take credit for great results. It is more important for the rich to get the credit than the payment. If great results can be traced back to your effort, everybody will want to do business with you.

This is not about magnifying the effort you put in to achieve the results. This is about making yourself responsible for the great results. When people see a desirable result and want to explore the factors that made the success possible, the rich make sure that their name is there somehow.

Regular people often do not pay attention to this. They just walk away as soon as they get paid for a job done. But the habit of collecting testimonials in business is very important. The best way to blow your trumpet is to let your results speak for themselves. The best way your results announce you is when other people testify to the fact that you were an instrumental factor in their success.

Great results can always be traced back to the rich. And that opens more opportunities for them to get wealthier.

## 7. They Show Up and Contribute at Top Events

Showing up is very important to success. The fact that the rich dress for wealth and success doesn't make much sense if they don't show up in important places. Business deals happen when the rich gather.

It doesn't matter if it is a wedding, a party, an art exhibition, or a theatre. Once the big business names are there, the game is on. Deals and contracts are often sealed in the informal setting.

Not everyone who goes to the opera house likes opera. But nobody minds it if it is going to make them some serious money. In fact, some love it because of the memories of the deals they have sealed from the opera house.

Do you think rich people do TV interviews and podcasts because it is fun? Absolutely not. They are showing up. They are positioning for opportunities.

The rich get richer from showing up at social events by meeting potential business partners and using informal occasions to seal deals.

◆ ◆ ◆

There are some other unusual ways the rich position themselves to be richer. But they are all based on one simple concept.
It is to make themselves feel the abundance of their wealth and
to make other people see it.

For the rich, everything is intentional. This is even more obvious with those who have been rich for a long time.

# PART V: LEVERAGE

They challenged me to a car race. So I brought my jet.

# CHAPTER 21: LUCK IS A SKILL

Life is just like a movie. And you are the lead character in your own movie. But sadly, most people are spectators in their own movie. They should be the lead characters, but they only look on and get tossed around by external forces.

Life is about taking charge and taking control. But many people don't want that. They might pretend to want it because it sounds good. But when the responsibility shows up, they become lazy.

Everybody feels lazy. But if you have a hot pursuit in life, it motivates you to get working even in those conditions.

I bet you know some lucky people. Maybe you even count yourself as lucky. But you want to know more about this subject. How do people get so lucky?

Luck is not a mysterious thing. And it is something that can be learned. Think about this:

Haven't you observed that it is people who think they are lucky that get lucky?

Those who always say, "I never get lucky," never get lucky. Luck eludes them all the time. When these unlucky people do get lucky, they look for something that will jinx it. And it doesn't take too long before they find it.

Meanwhile, when lucky people meet with bad luck, they often maintain their positivity. Luck is like a spirit animal. Those who embrace it get more, and those who keep questioning it get the little they find jinxed.

The more you think (and believe) you are a lucky person, the more luck will find you.

This is the first thing you should know.

## Take Every Ounce of Opportunity

One of the secrets to having good luck is taking opportunities. It is to never look at a chance and say, "I probably won't get it." Why would you not get it? It is because you think you can't.

This reminds me of the famous quote:

"If you think you can, you can. If you think you can't, you can't."

Life is that simple. Unlucky people don't take a lot of opportunities. They don't take chances. Now, I don't mean taking chances like playing the lottery. No! The lottery is a tax on people who are bad at math.

You seem qualified for the position, did you apply for it? The volunteer program seems like something that can boost your credibility and increase your professional circle, did you volunteer? They are looking for someone who will get the job done, did you express interest?

A fundamental aspect of luck is positivity. And positivity attracts opportunities. Lucky people take every chance that comes their way. Especially chances they seem not to be qualified for.

There are entrepreneurs who hire based on positivity. They rank positivity above skills. Skills can always be learned, but a positive soul brings good vibes and beautiful energy to the workplace. Positive people believe that they are lucky.

This is not the same as thinking that everything will come easy. Instead, it is the positive mindset that makes the hard work look easy. This is because lucky people actually believe in their ability to get the desired result. With the result in sight, the work is less burdensome.

Want to be lucky? Program yourself to believe you are lucky. Then take every ounce of opportunity.

## Luck Is When Preparation Meets Opportunity

All luck is not equal. Some strokes of luck are greater than others. But none of it is negligible. People who celebrate the luck they have become luckier. Those who look down on their good fortune become less fortunate.

Most business leaders, because of their experience, define luck as the point where preparation meets opportunity. And it is very true. Think about it: preparation meeting opportunity.

Preparation takes a lot of time. It takes months and years. If you start preparing when you see the opportunity on the horizon, you have started too late. Preparation begins when there is no trace of the opportunity yet.

But you prepare and prepare. You prepare because you don't know when the opportunity is going to come. Sometimes, you have 5 seconds to give the right response when the opportunity shows up. But if you haven't had 5 years of training and preparation, you will blow it.

Sometimes an opportunity seized in 5 seconds will take you beyond the point that usually takes 5 years. Many people miss moments like this in their lives because they didn't even notice it was their moment.

An opportunity will not come clinging to your feet and begging. Sometimes it acts like it wasn't there for you. Only those who have been preparing will recognize it and seize it.

Whatever your dream is, start preparing for it. If you want to be a great public speaker, start making those great speeches alone in your room at night. Project your mind into the situation. Act like you are already there.

Prepare now, because the opportunity will one day show up. And when you seize it, everybody will assume you are lucky.

## Prepare in Secret, Perform in the Open

A lot of people actually like to trace their results back to their efforts. They think it is a bad thing to be associated with luck.

They assume lucky people are lazy.

This is the reason a lot of people are quick to refute claims of being lucky, referencing instead all their hard work. That is not so good. Luck is like a spirit animal. The more you start attributing your results to hard work, the harder the work will become.

When people accuse you of being lucky, just smile and admit it. Say, "Yes, I am indeed lucky!" Not that luck just happened to you, but that you are a lucky person. Don't try to over-explain anything. Just answer the question. Don't lie about what you do. But always embrace luck.

When people think you are lucky, affirm it. As I said earlier, luck is positivity. Once everybody associates you with positive energy, many more opportunities will flow your way. Most people are superstitious. If you create good luck energy around yourself, everyone will want to do business with you.

Another way to make your good luck stronger is to prepare in secret. Have you ever seen people who want to lose weight go to the gym, and after their very first day working out they flood their social media accounts with gym pictures? Those are the ones who won't last very long.

There are lots of benefits that come with private preparation. I am a great proponent of privacy. It is always better when people don't see you preparing. You need concentration, and people would rather see the final result anyway.

I heard a top female entrepreneur say she practices a sales presentation privately about 50 times before going onstage. You would see her making her presentation onstage and exclaim, "Oh, she is such a natural!" No, she is not. You just never saw the bloopers.

It pays to prepare privately. But when you perform, make sure it is in the open. Don't perform in private. You need the world to see what you can do. It is when people see the product of 6 years of secret practice in 5 minutes of open demonstration that they say:

"Wow, you are so lucky to get all these results."

## Learn Parallel Skills or Subjects

To be different and distinguish yourself from the crowd, you need to add some spice to what you do. Most people go to learn about what they are doing in school. Personally, I am not a big fan of school, although I love learning. But going to school sometimes has its place.

If you have already found your path in life and you want to go to school more, I suggest you go study something that interests you but is unrelated to your skill or area of practice.

If you are a sportsperson, go take a course in leadership. If you are a chef, take a course in human psychology. If you are an engineer, take a course in communication and public speaking. If you are a TV personality, take a course in marketing.

Notice how divergent those combinations are. They are not totally divergent, but they aren't closely related either. Using thoughts learnt from another field of study to apply to your own field is actually a great way to stand out.

When you appeal to professionals from two different fields at the same time, those on both sides will call you lucky for getting along with the other side.

## Hide the Difficult Part

Unless someone asks you what the actual hard work entails, don't talk about it. Those who act like they really want to know won't like it in the end anyway.

As much as possible, hide the difficult part of the process. Make it look easy from an outside perspective. This releases a very positive energy from you. It is an energy that draws opportunities in your direction.

Imagine your workplace is facing a challenge. And they need an answer the next morning. And you spend all night working to resolve the situation. Don't shove it in everybody's face that you worked on the issue all night. People like to do this because it makes them feel good and they want to draw sympathy from others. Don't.

Act like getting the solution was no big deal. Then ask for the boss privately for some time off to go rest. If the boss asks why, then you can explain. But don't tell the others unless they really pester you. They don't care about the details anyway.

Hiding the hard work makes you look lucky. And people are not really interested in hearing about it, so why show it? Once people think you are lucky, they will expect you to continue to be lucky.

## Never Share all Your Secrets

It is good to share your secrets. Especially to an audience that deserves the information. However, you must never share all there is to it.

First, there are some of your secrets that are personalized. That is, they will only work for you. They will not work for someone else. If you tell someone else, they will try it, then it won't work for them and they will blame you. In fact, such people can even make you start doubting yourself.

The second reason is that this way you keep your secrets from being watered down. If you tell people, they will only point out theoretical flaws in your secret. If you don't tell anyone, nobody will attack you.

Do not try to help someone or bring someone up to your own detriment.

Sharing some of your secrets brings good vibes to you. But never share everything at once. If you have to share everything, then learn to talk in parables and puzzles.

Having some secrets you keep to yourself actually raises the value of the ones you share. When people have to use their imaginations to express the factors responsible for your success, you can be sure that the positive energy of luck will be included.

◆ ◆ ◆

Luck is a skill. And you can become good at it.

# CHAPTER 22: PROGRAMMING
# YOUR MIND FOR A RICH LIFE

T he missing link between your aspirations and the successful reality you desire is feeling rich (especially when you have yet to see the result you want). Your emotions are more powerful than you think. They not only affect your present, but they also affect your future.

Your mind does not live in time. Your mind does not function with time. So whatever you are feeling today is connected to your yesterday, today, and tomorrow.

Most people use their emotions to react to circumstances of life. They cry when they are sad. They laugh when something funny happens. They are excited when there is something exciting happening.

But that is not an optimal use of emotions. People who live that way are tossed to and fro by life's situations. They are always reacting; hence, life will keep happening to them.

Your life doesn't have to be this way.

## Your Feelings About Money Matters

You can be in the driver's seat of your emotions and of your life. You can achieve this by choosing how to express your emotions, regardless of what is happening to you or around you.

This goes on to affect money and finances. The emotions you let out with regards to money will shape your memory of money. You are teaching your mind how to respond to money with how you feel about it.

If you have negative feelings such as envy, anger, and bitterness towards money, it will be hard for you to make a lot of it. And there are many reasons for that.

The major reason for this is that your mind will record money as your enemy. And that is because of the negative feelings you have associated with it. When you try to make more of it, your mind will unconsciously push it away because it is an enemy.

This is why many are stuck in poverty. Their personalities have been shaped by the idea that money is their enemy. And they project their principles on others. This is why they are uncomfortable making a lot of money.

Most people know that thoughts are powerful, but very few understand that they are deeply connected with emotions. The power of thoughts is in the emotions you associate with those thoughts.

What creates your future experiences are the thoughts you spend time on and how they make you feel.

## You Become What You Think

This is a common saying that has been around for thousands of years. And yet, very few people pay attention to it.

Our thoughts shape our reality. There are millions of things we see every day. But the things we notice are products of our thoughts. For example, if you are thinking of buying a particular brand of car, you start to notice it is everywhere.

You may have thought the car brand was rare before. But once you set your thoughts on it, you start seeing it everywhere you go. That is the power of your mind.

This goes deeper. Your very personality is shaped by your thoughts. Your personality is formed from your opinion of yourself. If you think you are a good person, your personality will align with that. If you think otherwise, your personality will follow your thinking.

If you think you always make a mess of good things, your personality will likewise be shaped in that manner. And it even gets to the point of altering your abilities. For example, if you think you are a bad singer, you will continue to sing badly. But if you think you are a good singer and you believe it for long enough, you will actually become a good singer (even if you once had a horrible voice). I have seen this happen.

In my younger years, there were people I knew who always tried to sing beautifully. They were quite bad at singing. But they honestly believed they were good. Over time, their abilities shifted to match their beliefs and they became good at singing. I have also seen people who were great singers lose their abilities and become average once they started saying, "I can't."

It is the same with money and getting rich. Making the money is actually easy once the mental adjustments have been made. But lots of money will not change a person's thoughts about himself.

Your mind doesn't really know how much money you have. But there is a way you can train it to respond to money. Rich is a state of being, and it doesn't really depend on how much you have in your bank account.

If you think you are rich, you will be. If you believe you are rich, you are. It may only take some time for the money to get to your account.

Never let the opinions of others and society shape what you think of yourself. You become who you think you are.


## You Create More of How You Feel

Your mind records situations with feelings. And your mind is not swayed by your conscious thoughts or logical reasoning. It is based on your emotions.

When your focus is on something that creates a negative emotion, that will be what your mind continually makes you notice. And you will keep getting more of it.

There is a big difference between the statements "I am rich" and "I want to be rich." This is why so many people are stuck today. They want to be rich. As honest as that second statement sounds, it is a statement that you are lacking. If you think that way, you will always be in search of something and never see what you have.

The way to be rich is to internalize the statement "I am rich." You then make yourself feel the state.

The secret of getting rich is to internalize today the state of wealth you desire to have in the future.

Feel rich today. Forget about what you have or don't have. Feel rich today and your mind will create more of that experience.

## Your Mind Doesn't Know What Is Real

When you internalize a state, your mind doesn't know that you are just practicing. Every bit of it is real to your mind. This is why acting is the most dangerous job in the world. Your mind can't tell the difference between what is real and what is acting.

All your acts and behaviors over the years have been training your mind on what to bring to you. The more you focus on a certain thought with a feeling attached to it, that is what will keep coming your way.

If your mind doesn't know what is real, you can build a powerful impression of being a millionaire in your mind, even when your income is no way near that. But your mind won't buy it if you are just wishing for riches. Your feelings need to align with the thought.

Always remember that it is about feeling today like who you want to be tomorrow. That is how it works.

## Feel It Until You Are Convinced It Is Real

Initially, when you begin to practice being rich, it is going to feel awkward. There will be times when you just want to go back to your old vibes. But you have to keep going.

You may regress back into your old mold of thinking from time to time. But you must be relentless in your desire to internalize the feeling of your future today.

After many days of consistent practice, one day you will wake up and you won't be able to relate to who you used to be. Convince your mind that you have achieved your desired state today and it will bring you further proofs that you are in that state.

## Feelings Trigger Habits

When you are committed to using your thoughts and emotions to paint your future life today, habits that are consistent with that life will start to form. It will be easy to create those habits.

The reason for this is that you have changed the image your mind has about yourself. Therefore, your habits need to change to align with this new image of yourself.

Habits eventually create a lasting change. But you can't just change your habits without altering your self-image first. If you do, it won't be long before you go back to your old habits.

Your thoughts plus emotion create a staying power for any new habit you form.


## Feel Rich, Be Rich

Everything begins to change when you start feeling rich. Even those around you will notice the change. Don't let them get into your head and drag you back down.

Feeling rich involves your outward appearance, but it is not centered on your outward appearance. Remember, it is an internalized feeling. The outward cannot override the inward. The outward expression must always stem from what you are first comfortable with mentally.

Use your emotions to paint the thoughts of your future self today. It will get you rich in no time.

# CHAPTER 23: SECRETS ABOUT BANKS YOU SHOULD KNOW

Schools don't teach money. This is one of the major problems we have in today's society. The gross inequality in income and lifestyle that plagues this world is the result.

Nothing can completely close the gap between the rich and the poor. That is the reality. That gap will always exist as long as this world continues to be. However, the real culprit is the inadequacy of the merit system.

We designed the merit system to allow the best people to rise and thrive. However, the problems begin when that very system blocks the way of some people while giving others an effortless lift. This happens with the issue of money.

There is no education in schools about money. Part of the reason is if you are really qualified to teach it, you probably won't become a schoolteacher. Some say there is a powerful organization of people who won't let schools teach about money. But we all know that if you don't know how money works, you won't get far in life.

Banks are the custodians of money in this world. Almost everyone uses a bank one way or another. But not everyone knows how they really operate. You can choose not to care and focus on the broken merit system. But if you do, you have the same unfair advantages that the super-rich have.

Here are a few of some hidden facts about banks that the super-rich know.

## 1. Banks Have a Quota They Must Give Out in Loans Every Year

As far as the general public is concerned, the bank plays a simple game. They let people keep their money at the bank, paying them a small interest, and they loan that money out to other people at a slightly higher interest. The difference between the two interests is the bank's gain.

That sounds simple. It means the gain of the bank is dependent on how much money is kept in it and how much loans they give out. So, there are two ends that a bank aims for. The first is to increase the money that comes in. And this is achieved by having more and more people open an account with the bank (and use it).

The other end of growth is to give out more money as loans. So, what does that mean? It means when a bank is gaining a lot of customers, they also need people who will come and take out loans from them. And of course, they want people who can repay (as slowly as possible). The longer the length of repayment, the more the interest.

This is why banks have a quota they must give out in loans every year. Just as they have targets of new accounts opened, they have targets of loans. The only problem is that they don't publicize that as much. But rich people know this.

Of course, the bank turns down lots of loan applications (more on the reason why later). But they actually need them as much as they need the new accounts.

There is a theory that banks are more likely to accept loan applications made towards the end of the year. This is because in most cases, they will still be miles short of reaching their annual loan targets.

## 2. Each Bank Branch Has a Lending Limit

All bank branches are not equal. The titles of "regional manager," "branch manager," etc., are not mere titles. There is a limit to the amount a bank manager can approve for you. If the amount you are asking for is higher than what he can approve, you will be denied.

The interesting part of that is you may not be given a reason for the denial. And you will leave thinking there was something wrong on your side. In some other cases, if your deal is really good, the manager will transfer you to a superior to deal with. But they owe you no explanation to deny an application.

Another funny case is when the bank has already reached its lending limit for money loaned out. It doesn't matter how many references you have to back yourself up, your application will be denied. The bank cannot exceed its lending limit. The limit could in theory be extended, but it will certainly not be because you asked.

### 3. The Central Bank Will Always Bail Out Big Banks

This should be evident to everyone now. You could fight it and protest about it, but I doubt it will ever change. Instead of fighting it, why not embrace it? It is going to be there whether you like it or not.

There is the Federal Reserve Bank of the United States, the Bank of England, European Central Bank, Bank of Japan, and so on. They are the central banks of the world. And they will always save the big regular banks (commercial, etc.) when they are at the brink of failing. **With what?** Well, let's just say with the power that becomes money. You know that by now if you didn't skip chapters.

Big banks always get a bailout. As a result, they will always have money to shove out. You may not like that fact, but it is the world as we know it today.

### 4. Banks Don't Keep Money

Initially, banks were marketed to the public as a place to keep their money. Today, we use banks because they make it easy for us to use money anywhere and anytime. That is why they all have bank cards.

Even more interesting is the fact that banks are trying to discourage cash. So people have a lesser consciousness of loss when they exchange their money for anything. It makes transactions easy and life comfortable. But it also allows for more dangerous games to be played with money.

Banks don't keep the money. They make it circulate. Everybody knows that now. But they really don't know the implication of it. It means you are not the only one who has access to your money in the bank. The government now has some level of control over your money.

This is why the super-rich find ways to protect their wealth.

## 5. The Biggest Clients of the Banks Are Banks

Banks exist to serve themselves. Serving you is secondary. All the money brought into a bank becomes an asset of the bank. All the money loaned out of a bank is an asset of the bank. The game is almost "un-lose-able" for them.

This means the bank will always act in its own interest. The bank will never fight for those who keep their money in it. The bank fights for more control and interest. This is because when your money enters the bank, it is no longer yours. It is still your money legally, but now it is their asset.

The lending limit of a bank is always related to how much is deposited in it. And the ratio is always unfair.

## 6. Bankers Get a Yearly Bonus Based on the Performing Loans They Give

Obviously, this isn't all bankers. It would be those vested with that responsibility, often the managers. And this is not a bad thing.

The amount of the bonus is based on the loans given out. Of course, this wouldn't include bad loans, where the regular repayments are already getting missed. The catch here is that every banker wants that bonus at the end of the year. This is why they will more readily accept loan applications towards the end of the year (assuming they are still far from their target).

In most cases, they do this unconsciously. The banker at the beginning of the year has no pressure to approve loans. But towards the end of the year, they risk forfeiting their bonus if they don't approve enough loans. A greater motivator is the fact that no one wants to be known as inadequate or incompetent at their job.

Look at it this way: if you don't come and get money from the bank, the bankers are going to miss their yearly bonus. This is how the super-rich see it. And they keep walking into the bank to get every ounce of money they can. After all, they have the required collateral and credibility.

## 7. Banks Don't Give Money to People Who LOOK Poor

Bankers are the most impeccably dressed professionals in the world. And they are also trained (consciously or unconsciously) to see people based on their clothing and appearance. If you look poor, banks won't want to give you money.

Banks are big on judging people by their looks. That is why they are so meticulous with their own looks in the first place. They believe strongly in first impressions, and they are also won over by the first impression.

If you look like you need the money, they will probably not give it to you. If you look like you don't actually need their money, they will offer it to you freely. I have seen cases where the bankers come to ask people to take loans from them. It happens a lot. But they only go to those they think are rich because they look rich.

The only exception to this rule is if you have an account in the bank. Then they can look into your account to know whether you are truly rich or not. But if not, they size you up based on your appearance. And they can add up things about you pretty quickly based on what they are looking at.

The lesson here is to not walk into a bank looking broke, even if you are. This is why the super-rich display wealth in their manner of dressing.

The bank is only an institution. Ignorance is the enemy of the people.

# CHAPTER 24: THE BIG SECRET
# OF SUCCESSFUL BUSINESSES

No company has ever gone out of business because it had too many sales. None! The big secret of successful businesses is customers. Some refer to this as the market. Everything about your business can be wrong, but if the market wants you, that is the end of the story. You will always find a way to stay afloat.

I learned a great business lesson from one of the newsletter archives of Gary Halbert. He asked that if you have a shop that sells burgers and God gives you one wish concerning the business, what will your wish be? Think about it.

I thought about this and my mind started drifting in a lot of directions. I was thinking about what would give me an edge over everyone else selling burgers. Then Gary gave his answer and my mind opened up. What was his answer?

A hungry crowd.

If you have a hungry crowd, it doesn't matter how many competitors there are, neither does it matter if there are imperfections in your business system. A hungry crowd will always make your business successful.

◆ ◆ ◆

A business consultant had to advise a new restaurant opening up in a big city. He told the restaurant owners to fill up the restaurant every day with people. This included family, friends, relatives, whether they are buying something or not.

In a few days, the restaurant was getting filled by actual customers. Why? It is because:

Perception is reality.

If people fill up your restaurant every day, other people's perception will be that there must be something good about that restaurant that makes people keep coming to it. And they will want to try it out. Then you give them a wonderful dining experience and they will realize the restaurant is amazing. And they will probably talk about it to their friends.

◆ ◆ ◆

I recently had a conversation with a friend who is quitting his job and going the entrepreneurial route. He wants to build a social app. The first question I asked him is if he has a ready market.

There are some people who like to struggle and suffer. I don't. I have seen too many businesses with great potential fail. This is why potential doesn't mean anything to me anymore. There is only one thing that gets me excited:

A ready market.

◆ ◆ ◆

If you still do not understand the big secret of successful businesses at this point, I don't know what else to tell you. But if you do, you ought to know what to focus on.

Idea is trash. Execution is admirable. But a ready and hungry market is everything.

If you want to be an entrepreneur, find your hungry crowd. This is the first thing you need to figure out before anything else. Your business will not be successful if you are yet to find that hungry crowd.

One way to find your hungry crowd is to test and try things out on your own. Another way is to analyze the findings of other people and try to confirm them. Another way is to follow in the footsteps of someone or a business who already has figured out their hungry crowd.

Did you catch that?

# CHAPTER 25: HOW TO SECURE YOUR INCOME FROM THE UPS AND DOWNS OF THE ECONOMY

Have you ever wondered why some rich people just keep spending lavishly for years without ever having to work? Well, this is your answer: multiple income sources.

The secret of the rich lies not only in what made them a ton of money and made them relevant. It is also in the low-profile ways money keeps coming to them.

Most rich people are known for one or two things. But most of them have more than a dozen ways money comes to them. So, when there is an issue and their major income source gets blocked, they are still making money.

Most people exchange their time for money. Smarter people learn to leverage other people's time for money. But the smartest way of all is to have multiple income sources. This is how the rich insulate themselves from going broke.

Most rich people start out with a major business that makes

them a lot of money. But they know that if something should happen to that business, they would go under. So they set up another income source.

The purpose of this is to make sure that the failure of one business does not lead to their complete financial downfall.

Anybody can set up multiple income sources. You don't have to be super-rich to do it. The need for it is much more immediate in today's world.

We live in a fast-paced world where a whole industry can change in a matter of days. One invention can change a significant sector of the economy overnight. An outbreak can cripple entire sectors of the economy. That often leads to people losing jobs. And finding a new one is sometimes not easy.

But your expenses don't know you don't have an income anymore. The best way to get over life hurdles like this is to anticipate them. Set up multiple income sources.

**Multiple Sources, Not Multiple Jobs**

The first mistake people make when it comes to setting up multiple income sources is that they create more jobs for themselves. This is not about getting a second or third job.

The biggest problem the poor have is their mindset. It is so fixated on exchanging time for money. If the only way you think about money involves working hard for it, then you are grossly limited in how much you can make.

A job is an income source. But there are other income sources that are not jobs. Everyone gets started one way or another with a job, but other income sources should not be additional jobs. You only have 24 hours in a day, like everybody else. Also, there is a limit to how much wear your body can put up with before it breaks down.

True income security does not come from getting a second job. Setting up multiple income sources does not involve getting a second job. Think about it.

## Systems, Not Self-Employment

Another mistake people make about multiple income sources is that they think it is about creating a business. In their minds, what they call business is actually self-employment.

They call it a business, but it is actually no different from getting a second job. They just do not report to any boss in this case.

Self-employment is not the way to set up multiple income sources. You are limited by time, energy, and expertise. You can start your business through the self-employment route, but this is not how you should secure your income.

What you want to set up is a system. A system will require no effort after the initial setup. Or perhaps the additional effort is something you do regularly already.

Rich people can have as many as a dozen income sources. You can't achieve that with self-employment or side hustles.

A side hustle should go towards creating your dream business. You can grow multiple income sources from your side hustle, but your side hustle by its very nature is not a systemic income source.

## Make Money While Sleeping

The main criteria for judging a true income source that can safeguard your income security is this: can it make you money while you sleep?

If the answer is yes, then it is a good one. If the answer is no, you should reconsider it. Most rich people make money while they sleep. Their income grows based on the work they have done in the past.

Let's take an example to illustrate. Assume you write a song and record it. Then you license the song out so that you are paid royalties. That would be a good income source. You don't need to do anything extra for your song to continue to earn more money for you.

It is once you have things or assets like this, producing income for you even while you sleep, that you truly have income security.

Investments can also be applicable in this case. An example is a dividend-paying stock. Another is a real estate property that generates positive cash flow from rental payments.

A true income source should make money for you while you sleep. Note that capital appreciation is different from this. Income and net-worth are two different things. The focus here is on income and not on net-worth.

## Money Now, Not in the Future

Another deceptive pitfall many get trapped in is the promise of receiving money in the distant future. Your income has to be money in your pocket today. And it must also come in on a consistent basis.

It is not a source of income if it is a promise of income in the future. It is called passive income, not passive capital. Having passive capital is good, but it is not the same as having passive income.

If you have to sell something to get the income then, it is not passive income. It is only passive capital.

The game of income is very different from that of net-worth. Net-worth is the financial value of all you own. Increasing it doesn't necessarily mean your income is any better. Income security is only created by playing the income game and not by increasing the number of things you own.

## Estate Planning

When entrepreneurs have gotten very rich from their business, they protect themselves from losing it all by diversifying their income sources.

Big entrepreneurs whose income is tied to their net-worth try to reduce their dependence on the company they have created. However, in order to avoid an uproar, they have to be smart in the way they sell their stakes in the business. They call it estate planning.

This is how the rich protect their income. They do it all the time.

## Disconnected Multiple Income Sources

The secret to setting up a stable income security system is diversity. If the fall of one income results in the fall of another, it has defeated its purpose.

The income sources need to be independent of each other to be effective. One must not affect any of the others. All of them won't be of the same size, but they should be as disconnected as possible.

Sometimes we assume our income streams are disconnected. But an event later shows us that they are connected, and the failure of one income source triggers that of another. In 2018, two separate income sources I assumed were disconnected failed at the same time, triggered by the same event: a fall in the stock market. But even in the worst-case scenario, it should be impossible for all to fail at once.

You can only be sure that your income sources are disconnected if experience has proven it to you. Otherwise, you can only create another income source. More is always best.

## How Many Is Enough?

Start by targeting 12 sources. It can take a while to get there. But you will discover that as you go, more opportunities will be opened up to you.

I have income sources today that I didn't know were possible. As you get going, you will see more. You only need to make up your mind to have them.

Make a list and write down every possible income source you can have. Then do something towards securing each one of them.

This is how the rich protect their lifestyle through their income. It is by having income flow to them from multiple disconnected sources. And anybody can make this work.

# EPILOGUE: ONE HABIT THAT CAN MAKE YOU A MILLIONAIRE THIS DECADE

Nobody is going to get hurt by your becoming super-rich. In fact, the only way someone is going to get hurt is if you do not have enough money to get them out of trouble in time. You need to conquer your fear of success.

A popular US congresswoman said recently that billions of dollars are not made, instead, the money is taken. That is a very dangerous way to view money. If you see money that way, it will be impossible for you to have a lot of it. You will keep holding yourself back.

1% of the world population controls 99% of all the money. It is not because the 1% are greedy or smarter than everybody else. Instead, it is because they are the ones bold enough to believe they deserve the wealth.

You would be surprised at the number of people in the world who don't believe in being rich. They believe that one person's excess money is the cause of another person's lack of money. This is not true.

By the way, if you earn above $45K per year, you are in the 1% of the world that has 99% of the money. The super-rich are those in the 0.001%. If you have any negative beliefs about super-rich people, it will be impossible for you to get there. If you get there by accident, you will sabotage yourself (whether consciously or unconsciously) and bring your finances back down.

Until you believe that the world will be a better place if you are rich, your efforts towards getting rich will keep getting botched. You have to believe it. Not just to know it but also to be fueled by it. Think about it this way:

If you don't have the money, someone else will be in control of it. And you cannot choose what they do with it. If you have a cause you are passionate about, you should become rich so that you can support that cause with considerable funding.

Never trust the government to do the good you hope to see in the world. There are so many things that can go wrong. You cannot change the world as a broke person. You cannot change the world when you barely have enough for yourself and your family.

The best way to make sure that the good you want to see in the world becomes reality is by becoming rich enough to fund it. Being super-rich means looking away from yourself and your needs. Most people don't think about getting rich because they only think of themselves and their own needs.

Learn to think about others. The world will be a better place if you join the 0.001%. The habits that can make you a millionaire in this decade will not make sense to you until you have made this mental transition.

## A 10-Year Projection Is Better Than a 1-Year Projection

People often overestimate what they can achieve in 1 year, but completely underestimate what they can achieve in 10 years. For most people, 10 years ago they would not have even been able to fathom where they are now. In 10 years, your thinking changes and your paradigm shifts.

You can start a year thinking one way and end it thinking slightly differently. But over 10 years, your thinking cannot possibly stay the same. You will have a significantly different mindset, whether that change is positive or negative.

You can't really make an accurate 10-year plan. It is very likely to fall apart somewhere along the way. The reason is that life happens, thoughts change, and priorities change. A 1-year plan is very easy to make. But most of the time, people don't pull themselves towards their goals. Instead, they allow themselves to be pushed around by circumstances.

A 1-year projection is not very useful. This is because you don't need your imagination or belief for it. But a 10-year projection is powerful because it requires you to use your imagination. And that length of time is ideal for dreams to bud.

It may be hard for you to think you can be a millionaire this year. But it shouldn't be hard for you to believe you can be one this decade. A millionaire is not merely someone who has $1 million. I don't think of it that way. This is my broad definition of a millionaire:

A millionaire is someone who makes at least $1 million (net) per year.

A multimillionaire (in my opinion) is someone who does at least 10x of that. And it is not something far-fetched to achieve. In fact, you are smarter than some people who are already there. You just have to desire to get there and you will, eventually.

## Why This One Habit Will Work

I am making an assumption here. And you should know the assumption. My assumption is that you will get interested and hooked to content that shows promise for helping you better your financial life.

Whatever will change your life is going to come to you in the form of some new information. It could be something someone sent to your mailbox, it could be an ad you saw, it could be an interesting article title, and so on. But you must allow new (or even old) information like that to enter your mind and your world.

If you are not open-minded to new information, this may not work for you. Success is not magical. You cannot continue doing the exact thing you've done so far in your life and hope to suddenly end up with a magical result. There has to be a difference in some way. How can there be a difference if you do not allow new information into your mind? If you close your mind to the flow of new and productive information, I don't know what can help you.

This will work for you if you are a receiver or absorber of new (or refurbished) information that shows promise to transform your financial life.

## The Habit

The secret is very simple. And it is not new. But it is something that bridges the gap between wannabes and those who really become rich. I call it: fast implementation.

What is fast implementation? It is the habit of putting fresh knowledge to work instantly without any analysis.

Here is the guiding question:

What can I do with this piece of information now?

It is not what I can do tomorrow. Not what I can do next week. Not what I can do 10 minutes from now. It is what can I do now with this? What can you do with the information this very second? And you do it instantly.

Instant action is key. The imperfect action you take instantly is better than the perfect, well-planned action for tomorrow. And it is a habit you form.

The moment you get an idea, do something about it immediately. Talk to someone about it. Make an inquiry about it. Send an email, chat them up, walk into the store, do something about it now.

The more you do this, the more it becomes natural for you to do it. And it gradually grows into a habit. That habit can lead you to wealth.

Here is an exercise for you: what piece of information showed good financial promise to you recently? What are you going to do about it now? Do something now, not after you finish reading this book.

## Fail Faster; You Don't Have to Break Things

Mark Zuckerberg is known for his quote, "Move fast and break things." And it was a good quote until the Cambridge Analytica scandal, in which Facebook was a party to the violation of people's data privacy. You don't have to break things to get ahead, but you do need to move fast.

By move fast, I mean implement fast. A flawed prototype is better than an idea on paper. You have to move on from things that didn't work out well. And you must not allow the projects that didn't work out to make you procrastinate on the next one.

Not every piece of information will get you what you want. But don't just assume that a particular one won't work. Follow through before you toss it away.

Timing is a very important part of wealth building. You can almost never go wrong with fast implementation. Also, you are more prone to finish something that you've already started than something that is still an idea. Once you start something, the rest is not as difficult.

Implement first, then think.

## Are You Going to Commit Yourself to This Habit This Decade?

Doing is more important than getting it perfect. You implement first, then think later about how to optimize. This habit will lead you to bliss over the course of the next 10 years. The moment you see some useful information or get an idea, you do something about it.

Maybe you got a good idea from what you have read so far. What have you done about it? How can you implement it now?

If you commit yourself to this habit, you will be stunned at how much you will achieve over the next 10 years. Let me offer you an idea.

Find a space where you can write the words "Fast Implementation," where you can see them every day. That way, you will always be reminded of it.

◆ ◆ ◆

To your success in 10 years, cheers.

# IMPORTANT

My goal and motivation for writing this book is to inspire and influence 10,000 people (at least) to be millionaires before the year 2030. So this is not just a book, it is a passion project.

If you put the ideas and concepts from this book to work and you become wealthy, please do send me your story. I would love to read it, and your story will certainly inspire others.

Cheers.

P.S. If you are still trying to figure out where the riches are, let me save you from further stress. It is in you. Bring it out.

# ABOUT THE AUTHOR

## David Olarinoye

 David is gifted with the ability to make complex things simple. He educates people on the subject of money based on the experience of successful people and what has worked for him. He hopes to influence 10,000 people to become millionaires over the next 10 years. Learn more at his website, www.davidolarinoye.com